CURRENCY

DOUBLEDAY

D1058796

Life's a Pitch

▼▼▼▼▼▼

Then You Buy

Don Peppers

CURRENCY

DOUBLEDAY
New York London Toronto
Sydney Auckland

A CURRENCY BOOK
PUBLISHED BY DOUBLEDAY
a division of Bantam Doubleday Dell Publishing Group, Inc.
1540 Broadway, New York, New York 10036

CURRENCY and DOUBLEDAY are trademarks of Doubleday, a division of
Bantam Doubleday Dell Publishing Group, Inc.

Book design by Chris Welch

Icons by Jim Torok

Library of Congress Cataloging-in-Publication Data
Peppers, Don.
Life's a pitch : then you buy / Don Peppers. — 1st ed.
p.   cm.
Includes index.
1. Sales promotion.   2. Selling.   3. Persuasion (Psychology)   I. Title.
HF5438.5.P47   1995
658.85—dc20   95-13882
                                                              CIP

ISBN 0-385-47403-2
Printed in the United States of America
September 1995
1   3   5   7   9   10   8   6   4   2
First Edition

For Pamela

▼▼▼▼▼▼▼

Contents

Contents

Part II Pitching 51

▼▼▼▼▼▼▼

Part III Prospecting 179

▼▼▼▼▼▼▼

Introduction

▼▼▼▼▼▼▼

The Art of the Pitch

Rainmaker.

That's a fancy name for the person who drums up new business for an advertising agency, law firm, or investment banking partnership.

Since the early 1980s that's what I've been doing— pitching for new clients. I've taken part in or coached others in pitches for hundreds of advertising accounts— from Ocean Spray to Jiffy Lube, MasterCard to Maidenform. I've worked for Saatchi & Saatchi, Chiat/Day, Lintas:USA, and Levine, Huntley, Schmidt and Beaver.

As playing fields go, Madison Avenue is one of the toughest. The way ad agencies compete for clients may be the closest analogy to hand-to-hand combat in the business world. It takes place on a shifting, undefined terrain, with no hard assets—no patents, product differences, or distribution outlets—to cloud the debate. Several groups of white-collar professionals battle one another, each side armed with nothing but its own creativity and intelligence. The only way to win an advertising pitch is to out-think and out-hustle some of the country's smartest and savviest hustlers—professionals who have turned persuasion itself into a very profitable commercial enterprise.

The stakes are high. Winners pay bonuses, hire new people, and put commercials on the air that could make their agencies famous. Losers reduce staff, trim overhead, cut back. You do all you can to win.

I used to think that being a rainmaker at an advertising agency made me one of a select few. (Only a handful of people in the industry are full-time rainmakers.) But over the years I've become convinced that pitching is the most basic business skill. Everybody does it. All the time.

No matter what company you work for, in what industry, in what position, your success depends on your ability to persuade others to your own point of view. You pitch a prospective new employer to get a job. You pitch your boss to approve a project. You pitch your subordinates to live up to the spirit of your instructions, not just the letter. You pitch prospective clients to become current clients, or current customers to buy more. In your personal life you pitch your best friend to go to a particular movie, or your husband to agree to a vacation destination.

Face it: Everything in life's a pitch.

Every human interaction revolves around cooperation, collaboration, and persuasion—pitching. The ability to get other people to agree with you probably has more to do with success in business and life than even raw intelligence or creativity.

Even though we are all pitchmen at various times, few of us have ever thought seriously about the task of persuading others to our point of view. It isn't something we study in school. No one sets out to earn a doctorate in persuasion so they can launch a career in teaching it to others. Maybe they should.

This book is my personal lesson plan in persuasion, based on my years as advertising's best-known pitchman. It is filled with the principles I practice myself and impart to my clients, both in and out of the advertising business, all over the world.

Every pitch should be pursued along three dimensions —selling, psychology, and strategy. *Selling* means getting the basics right—like having an intelligent grasp of the client's business situation and overcoming any objections he or she may have to giving you the business. Using *psychology* requires probing the personality of the person you are pitching to and the corporate culture of his or her company. *Strategy* involves using, and bending, the rules of the game to outwit your competitors. Throughout the rest of the book I will identify the sections that focus on each dimension by marking them with icons—

 for selling;

 for psychology;

and  for strategy.

Incorporate these dimensions into your own approach to pitch situations, and I guarantee you'll be more successful. No one can win every time, but these principles will improve your odds. Always.

One

▼▼▼▼▼▼

Getting In

Chapter 1

▼▼▼▼▼▼

First Crash the Gate. Then Be Nice to the Security Guard

I hate obstacles, don't you? Nothing ruins my day faster than the word no. But if you're going to be in the pitch business, you're going to hear that word over and over. You can't let an obstacle like the word no, or the fact that you did not make the short list in a competition for a contract or a job, stop you in your tracks. If you honestly believe that you are the best person for the job, don't hesitate to try to get yourself reconsidered.

Often that means doing something unorthodox. But remember, each potential client or employer is unique, so you must tailor your approach to his or her needs and corporate culture. What is outrageously persuasive for one client will be outrageously inappropriate for another. The

secret of success is knowing the difference, and this re-
quires understanding the client's own culture.

▼▼▼▼▼▼▼

Word was out that Circuit City, the large consumer electronics retailer, was dumping its current advertising
agency. Pete Dow and I eagerly anticipated competing for
this $50 million account.

Our agency, Lintas:USA, was one of about forty agencies that received a questionnaire from Circuit City solic-
iting information about our operations. We filled it out
fully expecting to be selected for the next stage of competition. But when the list of six semifinalists was reported in
AdWeek, our name was not on it. Our agency hadn't made
the first cut.

This upset us because the six agencies on the list were
very much like Lintas. We were the same size and had the
same capabilities. Furthermore, our agency had a better
understanding of detailed, hard-hitting retail advertising
—the kind Circuit City would need most. We were sure
the electronics retailer had made a mistake by eliminating
us this quickly. So Pete and I hatched a plan to try to get
ourselves readmitted to the competition. It was a stunt
that would live forever in the memories of Circuit City's
selection committee.

We found out that the company had rented a hotel conference room in New Jersey, just across the river from New York City, to meet with the semifinalists. The selection committee had scheduled six one-hour meetings, beginning at seven-thirty A.M. This was the first face-to-face meeting with these agencies. Circuit City's plan was to eliminate three of them, and invite the other three to a final presentation round several weeks later. (We found all this out, and more, from our own source, who was close to the search process. More about how to do this in Chapter Twelve.)

The three members of the selection team planned to finish up by four-thirty P.M. the same day and return to their Richmond headquarters. This "lightning round" illustrated Circuit City's rapid-fire approach to corporate action.

We understood Circuit City's business philosophy well, and it was directly reflected in how its stores are run. The typical Circuit City is set up to maximize sales. The floor is laid out in a pattern something like a baseball diamond, with the entrance at home plate. Low-margin items—things that are put on sale regularly and advertised in order to draw traffic—are mostly at the opposite end of the store, clustered around second base. To get from the entrance to the sale items, a customer must either walk down the first-base line or the third-base line, turn a corner, and walk down still another base line, passing higher-margin items along the way.

Everyone at Circuit City is trained in selling. Their approach is gentle and consultative, but persistent. We decided to give the selection committee a taste of their own kind of selling. We would be gentle, but persistent. But we were outsiders. No one was asking us to sell ourselves to them. Circuit City didn't want to hear from us; they'd made that clear.

Pete and I executed the assignment ourselves, which was designed to show off our selling ability. It was tailored to Circuit City, selling experts who we felt would appreciate our chutzpah. We also had to be amusing and creative, so that no offense would be taken.

On the morning of the review we rented the hotel conference room adjacent to the one Circuit City would be using. We knew the company schedule, and we guessed that the team would have lunch—served by hotel staff, selected from a hotel menu—in between two agency presentations. We didn't know which agencies were showing up when, but we found out from the hotel kitchen that salad and cold cuts were to be wheeled in at exactly one P.M.

At 12:55, Pete and I had two piping hot pizzas delivered to our conference room from outside the hotel—one plain, and one with everything but anchovies. We paid extra to ensure that the pizzas were delivered to us at *exactly* 12:55.

During strategy sessions we labored over every detail. We wanted to walk in with something aromatic, so Circuit City's executives would immediately desire what we had to offer. We rejected hot dogs (too unhealthy), popcorn (no cachet), and submarine sandwiches (no aroma) in favor of pizza. With one plain and one "deluxe," we thought we could please all three selection committee members.

Two white-coated hotel service employees stood by in the hall outside Circuit City's conference room with one lunch cart of cold cuts, bean sprouts, and lettuce, and one of soda, bottled water, and coffee. At precisely one P.M., as Pete and I cracked the door to our own conference room and watched, one of the semifinalist agencies emerged from the conference room and the hotel employees began wheeling the lunch carts in. Dressed in our business suits and pushing our own borrowed hotel lunch cart with the pizzas, Pete and I walked in behind them.

As the irresistible aroma of two classic New York pizzas filled the conference room, the three Circuit City executives, still seated at their table, smiled and looked up from their notes.

"Great idea! Who ordered the pizzas?"

"All riiiight!"

We didn't know their faces and they didn't know ours. They thought we were from the hotel. As the hotel service people left, we put a clean plate in front of each executive and asked him what kind of pizza he'd like. Then we served a slice to each of them.

Once their mouths were full, we bent down to take three large binders out from under our lunch cart. They had our agency's name and logo, and included detailed information about Lintas—all the information we would have presented in person had we been invited.

Pete began a quick explanation.

"Hi, I'm Pete Dow and this is Don Peppers. We're from Lintas, and we brought you these pizzas because we wanted you to see how much we understand about the business you're in—selling."

They were already eating our pizza, so we figured they couldn't throw us out quite yet. With a warm smile and cheerful manner, Pete went on.

"We know what selling is all about. We know that if you really want to sell, you have to orient your whole company around it. You have to be relentless. You have to leave no opportunity on the table. That's the way we approach our own business, and that's the way we plan to approach yours, if you give us the chance. The binders contain all the facts and figures you need.

"Yes, we know your list of agencies has already been

published. But we don't believe any sale is totally lost until the customer buys from a competitor. You haven't bought yet—you're just examining the merchandise. If you want to change your mind, that's your privilege. You're the customer."

We didn't show them our work because the gift of the pizza only gave us permission to take a microsecond of their time. That's literally all we had—anything more would have killed the moment. Instead, we left them our samples so they could review them later. Then with a thanks for their consideration and their good sense of humor, we left.

Obviously a feat like this would have been totally inappropriate for a larger, more bureaucratic company like American Express, Procter & Gamble, or Pepsi. For Fortune 100 companies, it's rarely appropriate to try to get reconsidered on the strength of a wing and prayer. You're much better off if you are in the running from the start, so you need to be part of their consideration set before they even start looking for a new vendor.

If you're knocked off a corporate giant's short list, write a long, detailed letter with facts and figures backing up why you can help them. I guarantee they will read it—as long as it's about *them* and not just you. While it probably won't get you back in the running, it may put you in a better position the next time a job comes up.

With Circuit City we thought we had a reasonable chance of succeeding, and we were right. The next day Circuit City announced its list of finalists. To the amazement of our competitors on Madison Avenue, we were on it.

Three months and two meetings later, the competition was narrowed to us and one other agency. In the end, however, we lost. We lost "fair and square," as the other agency apparently presented an advertising strategy and several creative executions that the executives at Circuit City simply liked better than ours. When they called to give us the bad news, it was apparent that they admired our sales ingenuity so much they had almost given us the business anyway. Almost.

Chapter 2
▼▼▼▼▼▼▼

Making Contact

E very time you don't make it onto the initial list of candidates being considered for a job, a contract, a promotion, or a spot in graduate school, think of this event not as a failure, but simply as an additional step of effort required on your part to get what you want. This is just another obstacle, a mere problem to be solved, the same way you might solve any other problem.

There are as many ways to crash past these barriers as there are companies to deal with. What you need is ingenuity, guts, common sense, and a little bit of luck.

If there is one overriding principle at work in crashing a gate to get into (or back into) a pitch, it's this:

Find a way to make an offer to your prospect, and then make it an offer he simply can't refuse.

Make your offer so simple, so easy, so quick and imme-diate, so little time and trouble, the prospect has to be imaginative just to come up with any reason for not ac-cepting it. Do this right, and you'll have a good chance of getting a spot on the list after all.

▼▼▼▼▼▼▼

Calling on MCI

While I was working at Levine, Huntley, Schmidt and Beaver, we read in the trade press that MCI was review-ing agencies and that they'd already selected four agen-cies to meet with.

I tried to phone Judy, MCI's advertising director, but had no luck. With a little research I discovered that ev-eryone at MCI used an e-mail system called MCI Mail. I wasn't familiar with e-mail, which was an innovation at the time, but I learned that MCI mail was available out-side the company. So I got an account and sent her a message, which I knew she would get.

The message, which I sent very early the next morning, outlined all the reasons that Levine, Huntley should be included in MCI's review. Then I told her that I would call her at exactly 4:53 P.M. that day. (I had already checked with her secretary and learned that she had a meeting that should end at 4:30 P.M. and another one that should begin at five P.M., so I thought she would probably have a few minutes free at that time.)

Sure enough, at 4:53 she answered the phone herself. She was intrigued by the tenaciousness of the pitch. I had told her about some of the advertising we did. What I didn't tell her was that I was calling from the pay phone in the waiting area of her building. "I'm in your building now and I know you're in your office," I said. "I'd like to meet and discuss things with you."

She let me come up. We talked and I showed her a reel of commercials. She made us the fifth agency on her list of four.

This time I used e-mail, MCI's own system, to crack open the door to the company. Once I got the door open a crack, I was poised to take quick advantage of any opportunity that might arise. Had I not already been in the office building ready to meet on sixty seconds' notice, we may not have had a chance to meet with MCI at all.

Running After Reebok

Another time, when Reebok announced that it was searching for a new advertising agency, I was eager to enter the competition. Levine, Huntley, Schmidt and Beaver was just right for Reebok, but its marketing director, Sharon, would not return my calls.

So I decided to pay her a visit at Reebok headquarters in Boston. I was resolved to make contact with her if it was the last thing I did.

I didn't have a specific plan in mind, but I thought a prop might help me attract her attention. One of our commercials for Subaru had a life-size cardboard cutout of a nerdy-looking man called Schminsen. When I got on the shuttle to fly from New York to Boston, I carried Schminsen with me, wrapped in brown paper.

I arrived in Boston, went directly to Reebok's headquarters, and asked to see Sharon. I didn't have an appointment, but the security guard called her office to tell her I was in the reception area. So I sat down with Schminsen still wrapped up, and said I would wait for her to come out.

Finally, at about six-thirty P.M., after everybody was

gone, I asked the guard if she'd left. "Yeah, but she left by a different entrance," he said.

Next I proceeded to the Charles Hotel, where I had a reservation, checked into my room, and looked her up in the telephone book. There were ten listings that could have been hers. I tried all of them and finally got one where the answering machine clicked on and a recording said her name. And it sounded like her, or at least what I thought she would sound like.

I didn't leave a message, but I made a note of the address and headed straight to her apartment building—still carrying Schminsen. I couldn't get in the front door because there was no doorman. But I rang several buzzers until someone let me in.

I went upstairs and knocked on her door, but nobody was there. So I unwrapped Schminsen and left him in front of her door with a note pinned to his lapel.

"Sharon, I'm Don Peppers. I'm over at the Charles Hotel, and I'd like to have dinner with you tonight, or if not dinner, how about breakfast tomorrow morning? Or lunch, or dinner tomorrow evening? Please call me. I think it's really important that Levine, Huntley and Reebok at least get together."

Ten o'clock in the evening there's no call. Eleven o'clock there's no call. I wonder if this is going to . . . midnight. I fall asleep.

At four A.M. the phone rang.

"Is this Don Peppers?"

"Yes." It's her.

"I just want to ask you something. If I said in order for you to get this account you had to go to bed with me, would you do it?"

Luckily, before I had a chance to answer, she continued. "That's a hypothetical question. I'm amazed at your persistence. If I meet with you, can I keep the cardboard man?" She agreed to have breakfast that morning.

At six-thirty she came to my hotel and we had breakfast. We talked a lot and Levine, Huntley got its shot at Reebok.

We didn't win the account, but Sharon still has Schminsen in her beach house in Rhode Island.

How Far Is Too Far?

While I was relieved that Sharon's little wake-up question was hypothetical, it did raise issues worth thinking about if you're in the pitch business. How far should a pitch actually go? Where *do* you draw the line? I'm sure that's the point she was trying to make with her question in the first place. After all, I had found a way into her apartment building and left a note on her front door.

On the other hand, she already knew I had called several times and faxed her a note. After I flew to Boston to meet her, then waited unsuccessfully in her reception area for more than two hours, she evaded me by leaving through another exit. With all this, it wasn't as if Sharon and I remained strangers, even though we'd never actually talked on the phone. We were playing a little game of tag.

Naturally, I wanted her to know how serious Levine, Huntley was about getting in to see Reebok, but I had to do this with a sense of humor. We were an advertising agency known for irreverent, aggressive, smart-alecky creativity. I wanted to convince her we could pursue her business *creatively*.

If you begin chasing business as aggressively as this, you have to keep your sense of proportion at all times. Don't lose your bearings. There really are some things that cross the line. But by giving your quarry a chance to exercise some control over the situation you can often raise the stakes gradually, moving this line a little farther out.

Just remember: Never do anything in a pitch situation that would be counterproductive if it were done to you.

Don Peppers

Tips for Crashing Gates

1. Appropriateness is in the eyes of the beholder. Whatever tactic or stunt you're considering needs to be evaluated against the culture of the client whose business you're trying to obtain.

2. Make an offer your client can't turn down without behaving rudely. Your offer should cost the client very little time, accommodate any schedule the client wants, be at whatever location the client prefers.

3. Don't try to get everything at once. Get a phone call to make voice contact first, *then* get a meeting for a face-to-face contact, *then* get a decision to include you in the pitch. Never tell the prospect everything. Instead, let him discover each next step on his own, so he's not threatened by the magnitude of your ambition.

4. Have a next step in mind that can be agreed to instantly. When and if you have the opportunity to get someone's attention in a phone conversation, be around the corner, down the street, or right downstairs in the same building, if necessary, ready for a meeting on five minutes' notice.

5. Sometimes you have to wing it. Don't automatically assume your boss should approve every potential stunt, unless you think your career will be threatened if he doesn't. Your boss is almost certainly more conservative than you are. If you have the right relationship with him, you'll be evaluated and paid based on *what* you accomplish, not *how* you accomplish it.

6. Run your idea by a friend or colleague whose judgment you respect. Pick someone who knows your faults and won't hesitate to give you an objective evaluation (in other words, don't rely exclusively on a subordinate).

7. Better still, if you can, find someone who has already sold something to your prospect and ask his opinion. With a track record of success, that person may be able to help you fine-tune your pitch.

Chapter 3
▼▼▼▼▼▼▼

Gatekeepers

SECRETARY: *Hello, Ms. White's office.*

AGENCY EXEC: *Hi! I'm with the advertising agency Fishman, Wenslaus, and Partners. I'm just calling to follow up a package of material we had delivered yesterday. Do you know if Ms. White got our package?*

SECRETARY: *(looking around the office at piles of unopened packages from hopeful agencies stacked on the floor, the credenza, the lamp table, and the guest chair) What package was that, sir?*

AGENCY EXEC: *Oh, you'd know it. We sent a videotape enclosed in a fishbowl. It had live fish in it! Ha, ha! Remember now?*

SECRETARY: *(mentally replaying yesterday's scene, in*

which her horror-stricken boss asks her to have the fish taken somewhere else—anywhere else) Oh, yes, I do remember. Yes, sir, Ms. White did notice that package.

AGENCY EXEC: *Well, great! May I please speak with her now? Is she in?*

SECRETARY: *I'm afraid Ms. White is not available at present, sir. She's going to be in meetings all day today. However, your package has been forwarded to our search consultant, Mr. Screener, who is handling all inquiries. Feel free to follow up with him—would you like his number?*

▼▼▼▼▼▼▼

Gatekeepers, who serve as a shield for their clients or bosses, are another obstacle. If her client is looking for a new advertising agency, she protects the client from the storm of agency contacts, inquiries, and initiatives that will surely follow an announcement of a review. If her boss is an editor, she shields him from writers and agents who are looking for a publisher. If her boss has advertised a new position, she protects him from calls from eager applicants.

When a $20 million advertising account goes up for grabs, or is even rumored to be shaky, every advertising agency in the country goes on alert. Most of them immediately begin trying to contact the prospective client by phone or fax. Many send samples of their own work or their latest brilliant insights into the widget business by overnight delivery or personal courier. Most of these, realizing the battle is steeply uphill, try to get their packages noticed by including a clever device or gift, or perhaps by arranging an unusual delivery mechanism.

Within just a few days of any such announcement, the marketing vice president's office at the client firm is likely to contain fifty or a hundred letters, packages, videotapes, print portfolios, audiotapes, and miscellaneous chatchkas from ad agencies. Most of these packages will come from agencies she never heard from before. Her phone will ring constantly, as every agency executive in the universe tries to initiate his or her own intimate, personal dialogue with this hot new prospect.

Corporations often hire search consultants to cope with this deluge.

A key role for the advertising search consultant is to fend off unwanted inquiries and to protect his client from having to spend days on end dealing with what amounts to the world's most extravagant junk mail and telemarketing campaign. In the beginning the consultant may simply send out additional questionnaires to agencies who want to compete (after all, there's almost no downside for the client in having a larger number of submissions). In the latter stages of the search, one of the jobs the consultant sometimes performs is giving the bad news, as tactfully as possible, to the vendors not chosen.

Making Friends with Search Consultants

In my career as a rainmaker, I have found it very helpful to track and cultivate search consultants—especially the part-timers. Working as a search consultant requires no license, nor, in most industries, is there any organized market for this kind of service. Rather, consultants generally fall into one of two categories, either:

1. A professional, full-time consultant or consulting company dealing in very little other than helping companies evaluate and find vendors in a certain industry; or

2. An industry-experienced veteran, often retired, who is relied upon by people at a particular company, sometimes his former colleagues, for advice and counsel.

In the advertising business, the full-timers are generally more organized and formulaic in their efforts. And even though they are often more hostile to advertising agencies, once you get up to bat a couple of times with any of the full-time consultants, you'll be considered for future searches.

The part-timers are just people trying to help out a friend or do a job they never really had their heart set on to begin with. And there are many inexpensive, simple things you can do to cultivate a relationship with someone in this position.

Just corresponding with one of these consultants after participating in a pitch will create a great deal of goodwill that can ensure you have no problem getting listened to the next time, if there is a next time. Sending a search consultant a copy of an interesting questionnaire fielded by another consultant is another great way to make a friend. It also helps if you can think of some benefit for the consultant's other, full-time business (sending a job search to a headhunter who has managed an agency search, for instance).

None of these tactics will, nor should they be expected to, ensure your success. But simply getting him to take your phone call is all the victory you need, if your agency has a legitimately good story to tell about why it ought to be included on some prospect's list of candidates.

Another important reason for befriending the part-time consultant is that he is often more plugged in to the rumor mill, and he's less reluctant to share information. Given the chaos that often erupts whenever a pitch first becomes public, it obviously pays high dividends to be made aware of one just a couple of days—or even a few hours—in advance.

Going Around the Gatekeeper

If you can't make friends with a gatekeeper, you may have to go around him.

I was once called by an executive recruiter to discuss the position of president of a New York advertising agency. The recruiter was careful not to reveal the name of his client, but from the description of the firm, I thought it was probably the New York office of a Boston-based firm, Hill, Holliday, Connors, Cosmopulos. I knew Jack Connors a little, having met the CEO of Hill, Holliday at a number of industry functions, and I had already developed a reputation as somewhat of a hotshot new-business executive. I was fairly sure he knew and remembered me.

As it happened, before the headhunter called me I had already made up my mind to leave Levine, Huntley, and I was negotiating at the time for a business-development job with the much larger

Lintas, after being recruited by them for nearly a year. But the job of CEO was very enticing, even if the agency was smaller than Lintas. So I was highly motivated to get an offer for the spot.

The headhunter explained that his principal wanted an executive with substantial experience either on the creative side or the account-handling side, but that either background would be acceptable for the president of this office. Unfortunately, most of my experience was in business development, which includes some account handling but not much. On the other hand, business development is certainly an important background for a CEO at almost any firm.

In the end, the recruiter said he would take this up with his client and get back to me. A few days later he called to say I was not going to be considered for the position after all. What he told me was that his client simply wanted more account-side or creative-side experience for the position.

This news did not sit well with me, however. No phone call to me had been necessary to establish the fact that my professional experience lay in business development, and not on the creative or account handling side of the business. If this was such a mandatory qualification, then why contact me at all?

My guess was Jack Connors had instructed the headhunter to call me, and that this screening consultant had reported on my capabilities unenthusiastically. A possible alternative was that Jack had assigned the search to some other senior executive at the parent company and instructed that executive to contact me (through the headhunter), with the same result.

Remember, at this point I was still only guessing that the client was Hill, Holliday, although nothing the recruiter said had ever led me to doubt it. If it really was that agency, I was sure Jack Connors had put me on the initial list himself. He was the only person I knew there. But what could the recruiter have told him to terminate the discussion?

I decided to take matters into my own hands, circumvent the headhunter altogether, and simply call Jack directly. I called his office, introduced myself to his secretary, and asked if he was available, not saying why I was calling.

The next thing I knew, Jack was on the phone: "Oh, Don! It's great to hear from you! They told me you'd taken yourself out of the running for the position. I hope you're calling to tell me you'll reconsider?"

See what kind of games gatekeepers play to control events? I suppose it wasn't lying—technically

—to say that I had "taken myself out of the running," because the answers I gave regarding my lack of account-handling background verified that I didn't meet the specified qualifications, but that clearly was not the implication Jack had drawn from whatever he had been told.

So I said I had "decided to consider the position after all, if it was still open." He said it was, and the headhunter would call me again right away to set up some meetings in Boston. The next day the headhunter called and began setting up the series of interviews.

In the end it came down to me and one other guy. The other guy was apparently willing to work for considerably less money than I was, however, and he had a great deal of account-handling experience to boot, so they hired him. I took the job with Lintas, and in less than a year Hill, Holliday was looking for yet another president, having canned the man I competed with.

Chapter 4

▾▾▾▾▾▾▾

Warming Up Cold Calls

C old-calling—making contact with people who've never heard of you and have no reason to take your call—is one of the most powerful tools a business developer has.

When I worked at Levine, Huntley, Schmidt and Beaver, a large part of my job was making cold calls to marketing executives and senior officials at companies with big advertising budgets. Cold-calling was productive for our firm because I often reached executives who admired our advertising but were not familiar with our agency. Our work was very creative, and therefore memorable, but our firm was small and not well known.

It's not always easy to talk with people inside a com-

pany. Your goal may be to get into a pitch or to win a computer servicing contract, but first you have to get them to pick up the phone to talk with you.

▼▼▼▼▼▼

Touching Up Maybelline's List

I was in charge of the business-development efforts for Chiat/Day Advertising when Maybelline was bought by an investment banking firm in a leveraged buyout. The new owners announced they would be putting the advertising account up for review, and a call to their firm soon turned up the name of the partner who was in charge of operations at the newly acquired company. However, I couldn't get him to return my call, and it was apparent that the review was happening without our participation.

We knew no one who had any kind of link to this investment banking firm, or to the particular manager we were trying to contact. Not only that, but while the firm had a clear public profile, there was almost no publicly available information at all with regard to the company's business views, its outlook, or strategy.

One bit of information turned up that proved very useful, however. We found a brief paragraph about our prospect executive in *Who's Who.* We learned he was trained as an economist, and had migrated into investment banking. As it happened, my very first job in the business world, when I left the air force, was as an economist.

So I faxed him a letter that simply began with the words "We have something important in common. We are both economists." The rest of the one-page letter explained that a good economist would describe the process most firms go through in selecting an advertising agency as "satisficing"—an economics term for reviewing one option at a time until a satisfactory option is uncovered, and then accepting that option. This, I said, was the process Maybelline was following by adhering to a normal agency review process.

A better approach, as any economist knows, would be "optimizing"—reviewing the universe of all practical options and then selecting the best of this universe. In ordinary life, when options are almost unlimited, it's impractical for a decision-maker to optimize. But in an agency review, when only a few dozen practical options exist to begin with, optimization would be a much better decision-making method than satisficing.

This was the entire argument in my letter. We faxed it to him in the morning and he called us that afternoon to schedule a meeting the next day.

Mastering MasterCard

During my third year at Levine, Huntley, we read in the trade press that MasterCard was looking for a new agency. I called the consultant who was in charge of the MasterCard pitch, and was told that the people at Master-Card were looking only at agencies that billed $150 million or more. That criterion eliminated Levine, Huntley because we billed only $120 million.

Not ready to give up, I learned that the woman in charge of the search at MasterCard, Joanne, was a high-profile professional woman whose name was in the press a lot. It was very difficult to get her to pick up the phone and talk to us, because lots of people were calling her and she had a bevy of call screeners working for her.

After studying a speech she'd given a few months earlier, however, I sent her a three-page Mailgram listing the primary reasons MasterCard ought to include Levine, Huntley in its review. I replayed many of the themes from her speech, changing some of the thoughts around, but not enough to disguise them too well. I intended for her to realize we read her stuff and had digested what she said. We wanted her to recognize her own message. I didn't tell her in the Mailgram where we got the material —which was public knowledge—but I wanted her to see somebody out there was listening, and it was us.

She obviously wanted to be famous; I wanted her to think of me as a fan.

Lo and behold, we did get the call back, and we became the eleventh of ten agencies competing for Master-Card's business.

When we did further research into Joanne's background, we discovered she had worked for Werner Erhardt at est and was a big proponent of his training. Rumor had it that the tag line "master the possibilities"—a phrase that figures prominently in Erhardt's training—had been written by Joanne and urged on MasterCard's advertising agency, William Esty. (Usually it's the agency that writes the tag lines and advertising copy.)

So before our meeting with the MasterCard group, we went through our whole presentation, which included case studies of our work, and "est-ized" it. We replaced passive verbs with active verbs. We eliminated all prepositions. We converted our presentation to an action-manifesto for MasterCard. Our slides and charts stressed that MasterCard was an organization that could master its own universe, and its own possibilities for competitive success.

We succeeded in making it into the final round, when

we were up against just one other agency, SSC&B, a firm about ten times our size. Ultimately, however, we lost when the president of MasterCard chose SSC&B over the nearly unanimous objections of Joanne and her marketing team. (SSC&B later changed its name to Lintas, and it was immediately after the MasterCard pitch that they began trying to recruit me.)

Chapter 5
▼▼▼▼▼▼▼

The Short List

Just because you can crash the gate once in a while doesn't mean it's the best way to get in the door. The best way to earn a coveted spot on a prospect's short list is the old-fashioned way: to earn it.

If your firm is selected to receive a review questionnaire or request for proposal (RFP), or if you are called in for a job interview, you're in contention for the short list. Making that list elevates your status from candidate to serious contender.

Many RFPs run to dozens of pages, with detailed requests for information on everything from a company's work history and client references to its financial systems. Advertising questionnaires, for instance, frequently ask about costs and profit margins by size of account. Preparing answers for these interrogatories can require book-length documents.

The first thing to remember is that the primary job of the person or committee drawing up the short list is to narrow the field. Just as one typo on a résumé can rule out a job candidate, one error in your RFP could cost you your spot on your prospect's list.

The overall guiding principle about written correspondence between an applicant and a prospect is this: It is not used to select winners. It is used to eliminate losers.

No matter how much original thinking you put into any written document, winning the account, a job, or a spot in next year's graduate class almost always will still require a face-to-face meeting. On the other hand, one or two mistakes will probably be sufficient to get you eliminated from the pitch. Therefore, you must create an error-free document. (See "How to Create an Error-Free Document," page 45.)

What an RFP Can Tell You

When you begin working on a request for proposal, a questionnaire, or any other written document required by your prospect, **write down your communications objectives *first*.** What are the key points you want to make? In any pitch, for any prospect, you and your colleagues should first agree on your own firm's goal or point of view. Writing your communications objectives down before working on the RFP is the best way to avoid lack of coordination later.

Then consider the method by which the responses will be evaluated. Every client will have a system for reducing the voluminous amount of reading involved, but most companies adopt one of two methods: either one person will be responsible for the initial screening, perhaps with some oversight from another manager, or a team will do it.

If the responsibility falls to one person, you can bet that *this person will not read every word in each of the responses.* At some point she is likely to take a look at the two-foot-high stack of responses on the credenza and ask herself which question *has to be answered right* for a competitor to be considered. Then she will read that single item in each response, eliminating those who don't get it right. She'll create two piles, one for rejects and one for those who gave the required answer to the most critical question.

The next step may be to choose the next most important question, and so forth, until she has eliminated all but a manageable pile of proposals—probably five or six, and almost certainly no more than ten.

Some teams will approach the task in the same way. Other teams will divide up the questionnaires among team members, ensuring that someone is responsible for reading every word of every document. A scoring sheet will often be used to compare the evaluations different readers have given for each response.

When you first get a questionnaire, spend time thinking about how it is likely to be evaluated. A fast-growing, entrepreneurial company, or a company that operates in a fast-paced retail environment, is likely to assign all the questionnaire responses to a single re-sourceful individual to make the first cut. A larger or more mature organization, likely to be managed on a consensus basis, will usually assign a team or committee.

Make your best guess as to which question is absolutely critical to the prospect's evaluation of responses. You should also think about how you would create the scoring system if you were doing the evaluations.

Always ask the prospect how responses will be evaluated. You should do this for two reasons: First, the answer will help you prepare your response. Second, *and far more important*, when you learn how responses will be handled, you'll gain insight into how decisions are made at this company—insight you will need later, to prepare for the actual pitch meeting.

How to Complete a College Admissions Application

A similar method can be used for filling out applications for college, or graduate school or law school, or for any other activity in which a set of questions has to be answered in writing, as long as you remember one important difference:

In many cases, a written application will be used not just for screening, but for final selection as well.

If a questionnaire response, RFP, or application document is being used just for screening, then it's important not to make mistakes, and not to take too many risks. All you want is not to get eliminated.

But if the document is going to serve as the final criterion for selection—as is true, for instance, with almost all college and university applications—then in addition to not making mistakes, you have to use the document to *position* yourself relative to the other applicants. This can mean taking a few risks, in order to look "unusual."

Consider the college admissions process, for instance.[1] The typical college has tens of thousands of applications for thousands of admission spots. And what is a college interested in? You may be surprised to know this, but most colleges don't look so much for well-rounded *students* as they do for well-rounded *classes*. This contrasts to the way a law firm or ad agency might be selected. But a college is selecting thousands, or at least hundreds, at a time.

The typical college admissions committee appoints junior and midlevel staff members to read every application. The staff person may take fifty or one hundred applications home with her each evening, intending to read every word in every one of them, but of course this rarely happens. Instead, the reader will do just what a corporate executive would: concentrate on the most important points first, in order to make the task more manageable.

After selecting based on grades and test scores, there will probably still be several times as many applicants who meet a college's admissions requirements as there are spots to award. So now how does the selection process proceed?

[1] For an excellent description of these concepts as they apply to college admissions, see *Getting In* by Paolo de Oliveira and Steve Cohen (New York: Workman Publishing Co., 1983). I'm indebted to my friend Steve Cohen for his insights.

Typically, the admissions staffer has to present her assessments of the applicants she's screened to a more senior committee of admissions people. To do this, she needs to have handles for the applicants she's going to discuss. She has to have a way to talk about the applicants before the selection committee. "This is the girl who parachuted" or "Remember, this is the boy who plays violin in the city's youth orchestra."

The way you position yourself if you're trying to get into college is by doing something unusual—out of the ordinary. Ideally, of course, it will be some unusual sort of accomplishment or achievement, but it doesn't have to be. Earning a scuba license at the YMCA, or volunteering in the local Salvation Army center every week, or starting an amateur astronomy club, or running a business cleaning barbecue grills every spring—any of these activities would probably be singled out when your application is reviewed.

How to Create an Error-Free Document

Here are my eight rules for written correspondence with a prospective employer, vendor, graduate school, or client:

1. Support your case by using numerous examples.

Any assertion is more persuasive when accompanied by specific examples and anecdotal evidence. Whether you are alluding to your company's capabilities and past accomplishments, your insight into the market or the competitive situation, or your previous academic training, punctuate your argument with brief, illustrative examples.

2. Make all your answers *specifically relevant* to this prospect.

Every answer to every question should include a specific reference to the prospect's situation. Every answer should contain the information necessary to fill in the blank: "This is relevant to the XYZ Corporation or ABC Graduate Program because _____." (*Don't* actually write this sentence into your document, but the reader should be able to complete this kind of sentence for himself based on what you do write!)

3. Differentiate, differentiate, differentiate.

Identify everything you can do faster or better or more creatively than your competitors. Then announce it, illustrate it, prove it, and make it relevant to this particular prospect.

4. Be brief.

Any answer that takes more than one single-spaced page had better be packed full of relevant examples and concrete facts. Resist the urge to bulk up your responses to essay questions. Concentrate instead on hammering home your communications objectives.

5. Be consistent.

In some ways the invention of word processing has been a blessing for paper-intensive exercises like this. In other ways it has been a curse. You'll probably find yourself taking ready-to-use language from previous RFPs and other documents and inserting it in this one. Make sure you proof your RFP for consistency from section to section.

6. Use perfect grammar, spelling, and punctuation.

Writing an RFP response, or a pitch letter, is like a résumé in search of a new job. Any grammatical awkwardness, tYpos, mispellings, style inconsistencies or punctuation errors, are grounds for immediate elimination in the twisted minds of some prospective clients. If you aren't a good enough proof reader to pick out the 9 errors in this paragraph, then get you're written materials read by some one who is. (For corrected paragraph, see *Answers to Grammar Quiz,* page 50.)

Some guidelines:

▪ *It is absolutely imperative that the prospect's name, title, and company name be properly spelled and styled. It is always a good idea to call the pros-*

pect's office and confirm the details. Also, how does the firm refer to itself in the colloquial? Do they say "Nestlé" or "Nestlé's"? Is it "KMart," "K-Mart," or "K Mart"?

- *Active voice is almost always better than passive. "We delve into all aspects of a client's business" reads much better than "All aspects of a client's business are examined in detail."*

- *Avoid/minimize excessive use of the slash (/), or your materials will look overly bureaucratic/weird.*

- *Sentence fragments. In general not a good idea.*

- *Avoid excessive capitalization. Proper nouns and the word God, when used to describe a Supreme Being, can be capitalized. But the words* agency, client, firm, *and* company, *as well as most job titles, should remain lowercase, unless your intent is to imbue these terms with some kind of religious significance. It makes for easier, less formal reading.*

- *Avoid grandiosity. Always opt for the simplest, most straightforward language. Use* first *and* second *rather than* firstly *and* secondly, *for instance.*

- *Hyphenate properly. Watch out for dashes that come out of the word processor as hyphens, and vice—versa. Use hyphens, generally, to link word strings that are used as adjectives. The statements* We are an agency that delivers full service *and* We are a full-service agency *are both correct.*

7. Avoid fluff.

Words such as *breakthrough* and *brilliant* tend to show up frequently in any advertising agency's description of its own work. Similar words probably crop up in other industries. But the *only* time you should feel free to include a laudatory comment about your own firm in an RFP response is when the comment has come from someone else, whom you are quoting—a quote from a magazine article, a current client, or a prominent personality.

8. Make sure your document is readable.

Put yourself in the place of a prospect who receives five or ten or even fifty lengthy, densely written applications. Now he has to read them. My rule of thumb: A reasonably bright fifteen-year-old should be able to get through the meat of your response in a single evening without getting confused, falling asleep, or chuckling uncontrollably. After he finishes reading, he should be able to tell you what your communications objectives were.

Answers to Grammar Quiz

Writing an RFP response, or a pitch letter, is like **sending** a résumé in search of a new job. Any grammatical awkwardness, **typos**, mis**s**pellings, style inconsistencies or punctuation errors **[comma deleted]** are grounds for immediate elimination in the twisted minds of some prospective clients. If you aren't **[normal space]** a good enough proo**f**reader to pick out the **nine** errors in this paragraph, then get **your** written materials read by someone who is.

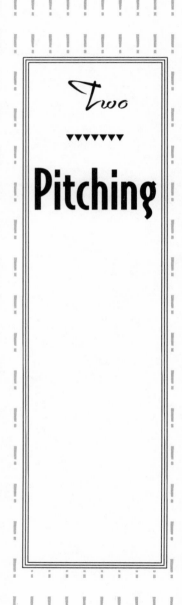

Two

▼▼▼▼▼▼

Pitching

Chapter 6

▼▼▼▼▼▼▼

Selling, Psychology, and Strategy

Pitching is like juggling, but instead of keeping three oranges in the air, you are balancing three disciplines: salesmanship, psychology, and strategy. It is essential to develop your skills in these areas. All the psychology and strategy in the world won't help you if you can't close a deal. Strategy and salesmanship are useless if the potential client just doesn't like you.

This chapter will give you an introduction to each of the three disciplines. Following chapters will tell you how to manage each area as you develop your pitch.

 **Selling**

Walk onto any car lot in the world and sooner or later your salesman will try to uncover your reasons for *not* wanting to buy a car from him. He's taking the first step toward making a sale: Find out why someone doesn't want to buy and then answer those objections.

Overcoming objections is the first step in any successful pitch.

Most people prefer to counter a prospect's objections to hiring them at the end of their pitch. The typical ad agency team, for instance, tries to impress their prospect with their creativity or marketing plan before handling objections. "First let's make them love us. Then we'll win despite their objection." Sound familiar? It's typical of many selling teams in many industries.

But it's not the right approach.

Attack and neutralize any objections your potential client has to awarding you the business first. The reason is quite simple: If there is some obstacle that seems insurmountable to her, she won't hear anything else you have to say until you deal with it. She won't hear your brilliant solution to her problem. She'll be distracted when you bring up your terrific pricing terms. She won't care about the insightful, experienced account team you've assembled.

In the back of her mind—probably not even consciously—she'll be thinking that your argument doesn't really count, because there's an overriding reason she can't give you the business anyway.

As long as an obstacle blocks your path, you won't ever get the prospect's full attention.

If you haven't spent much time thinking about pitching, it's easy to get depressed every time your prospect reveals a new objection. Successful salespeople don't think of a prospect's concerns as hurdles, however. They are beacons. If you know a person's objections to giving you business, then you have a map showing the route to success.

Objections aren't obstacles. They are signposts.

Psychology

Equally important to winning a pitch is your ability to know what makes your prospective client tick. I divide this into a two-step process:

First, you need to understand the psychology of the

company. Attempt to learn what it would feel like to be immersed in your prospect company's corporate culture.

Second, understand the psychology of the individual decision-makers at the company. Try to uncover the emotional, nonrational components of their decision-making. Emotional reactions are usually far more influential than rational arguments.

In pitching, listening is more important than talking. A successful pitch involves an exchange of thoughts and ideas. Someone has to do the persuading, and someone has to be persuaded.

The only way you'll ever be able to achieve your goal— changing the other person's mind—is to understand what is going through that mind.

Since listening doesn't come naturally to me, I've had to train myself to listen more carefully. I've made the listening process into a game, in which I try to decode the conversation while the other person talks. I look for clues —keys to winning the pitch. The more the person says, the more clues are revealed and the better prepared I will be to persuade this person later.

One way to zero in on corporate culture, for instance, is to identify unique characteristics of the vocabulary used at the company. "Key words" are the words you pick up in conversation with your prospect. You know you've identified a key word when you hear it used in a unique way, or used repetitively, or used by a number of executives at the firm to describe a particular problem or issue.

In addition to trying to analyze the corporate culture, to win a pitch you have to analyze the *people* involved in making the decision. Remember that companies and organizations are just legal conveniences. They have no brains of their own. Only people make decisions, and usually they do so for reasons even they themselves don't fully understand.

It's foolish to think that a subjective process such as making a group decision on awarding an account can ever be made into a totally rational, objective process. It can't. Understand this simple fact and you'll be way ahead of most of your competitors.

 **Strategy**

As a strategist, your first task is to differentiate yourself from your competitors. The easiest way to do this is to do something totally unexpected.

Violate the prospect's expectations, and chances are you'll be remembered for this more than for anything else. The prospect's managers will then refer to you by a label that identifies whatever you did in your meeting that

Don Peppers

was unusual and surprising. "They were the ones who did ____, right?"

When you're trying to decide how to stand out, think about the process that went into selecting your set of competitors. In almost any industry there are a large number of firms who would be interested in competing for a worthwhile account. But the prospect has already gone through some sort of elimination process to select a particular set of competitors.

This was not a random process. If you examine the set, you're likely to get a good picture of the prospect's preferences. What do you have in common with your competitors? The answer to this question will tell you why you're on the list and what the prospect is looking for. Then figure out how you can meet or exceed those expectations, while doing something different enough to stand out from that crowd.

Second, keep in mind that a pitch is a zero-sum game. *There must always be a winner, and there can be only one.* Knowing how to pitch means remembering that the contest will be graded on a curve. There will be only one student at the top of the class.

So, being best is better than being perfect. No matter how difficult a pitch is, or how rushed, there still has to be a winner. Size up your competitors—they're the ones you have to beat.

Sometimes you'll have an opportunity to change the rules or mess up the playing field. (One of my favorite tricks is to convince a prospect to move the deadline up. See Chapter Eleven.) Even if it will handicap your own effort, ask yourself if it will hurt your competitors more. If so, do it!

Chapter 7

▼▼▼▼▼▼

Overcoming Obstacles by Frontal Assault

 Remember: Overcoming objections is the first building block of a successful pitch.

Shortly before I was hired to direct Lintas's business development, Sitmar Cruises, a client managed by the agency's Detroit office, was acquired by its competitor, Princess Cruises.

The Princess brand was painted over the Sitmar name, and our agency was offered a "courtesy" opportunity to compete for the entire account, some $40 million worth of advertising and promotion.

This was my first assignment at Lintas, and it was going to be very tough. Courtesy reviews like this rarely result in dislodging the incumbent agency, in this case, Tracy-Locke.

We prepared for this contest by first listing all the objections Princess's management might have to awarding its account to Lintas.

We listed quite a number of reasons Princess would prefer Tracy-Locke over our firm. First, all the inherent advantages of incumbency went to Tracy-Locke, an agency with whom Princess had worked and grown comfortable over the last several years. The advertising itself, while not remarkably "creative," in the jargon of ad agencies everywhere, had nevertheless been fairly successful. The *Love Boat* TV series had been shot on a Princess ship, so Tracy-Locke used Gavin MacLeod, the *Love Boat*'s captain, as a spokesperson in Princess's advertising. Although this advertising theme was becoming a little worn, it was still producing results.

In addition to these factors, there did seem to be one overriding obstacle that was a major hindrance to our getting the business.

Princess's headquarters was in Los Angeles. Tracy-Locke had a number of clients and a full-service office in Los Angeles, with creative, research, and media-buying staff in place. But Lintas did not have a full-service office in Los Angeles, nor would it be economical to open one. Even though Sitmar's headquarters had also been in L.A., Lintas had never maintained more than a field office on the West Coast.

We learned that Princess's management—particularly their CEO, who had just been imported from the British parent company—felt that having a full-service agency office "just down the street" in Los Angeles was absolutely essential to getting good advertising. Our rivals at Tracy-Locke had certainly nurtured this idea, of course.

Although our Los Angeles office was not a full-service office, it did employ some fourteen managers (mostly account executives) who worked full-time on the Sitmar business, and our client had never complained. If we lost the pitch, these fourteen people, among others, would lose their jobs. This was truly a life-or-death pitch.

Even without this particular obstacle, it was going to be an uphill struggle to dislodge Tracy-Locke. But we did have a great creative idea and a very smart, information-rich business plan to show them. We were going to demonstrate a database marketing and targeting system with a computer terminal we would set up in the presentation room. We also had an innovative way to refresh Gavin MacLeod's role in the advertising. We were confident our agency had a better insight than Tracy-Locke into what it would take to build the newly merged cruise line's business successfully.

Most of the executives on Lintas's pitch team thought it would be best to present the advertising ideas and the database marketing plan first—thus weakening the resolve of Princess's management to insist on a Los Angeles field office. We knew the database demonstration would be particularly persuasive.

But after discussion we agreed that if we wanted a serious chance at winning the business we had to overcome our prospect's objection first, so they would be capable of hearing what we had to say when it came to strategy and execution.

Basically, we had two options. We could knuckle down and establish a much larger, full-service office in the city —an office with not just account-service employees, but also creative, media, and research staff as well—an extraordinarily expensive option. Or we could meet their objection head-on and simply overcome it. We could persuade Princess's management—specifically the company's CEO and his immediate deputies—that they were wrong. We could change their opinion. But we knew the only chance we would have of even meeting the CEO face-to-face would be in our final presentation, which he was scheduled to attend.

We prepared for this meeting first by talking to every friendly colleague and associate of the CEO and his deputies that we could find. We tried to learn as much about each of them as possible. We quizzed the people who knew them to determine whether and under what circumstances they might be persuaded to change their minds, even in front of subordinates.

Then we hatched a plan for the presentation designed to appeal directly to the CEO and overcome the "full-service office" objection with the strategic equivalent of a frontal assault. We knew it was the only way to win the business, and it had to happen first, before anything else could possibly be effective.

So Pete Dow, the ebullient president of our Detroit office, opened the meeting by putting up a board on which was drawn this diagram:

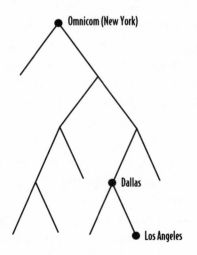

Figure 1

Many advertising agencies, he said, are organized with this kind of structure. Each node in the structure is a full-service, stand-alone advertising agency or agency group. It's easy to manage an agency network this way, said Pete, because every office can be held fully accountable for profit and loss. Buying a new agency or agency group is easy, too—just graft it on to the chart and it can be held accountable in the same way, and evaluated according to the same standards, as every other agency in the network. This is how Tracy-Locke is organized, he said. He circled one of the nodes and wrote "L.A." on it. Then he circled another node and wrote "Dallas" on it (Tracy-Locke's other principal office). He circled the node at the very top of the chart and wrote "Omnicom," the name of Tracy-Locke's mega-agency parent corporation.

But, Pete said, this is not how Lintas is organized. He put up another chart:

				Detroit	
	New York				
			Atlanta		
		L.A.			
				Miami	

Figure 2

Lintas is organized this way, he said. Particularly in an age of air travel, faxes, and e-mail, this seems to be an increasingly efficient way to organize a company for doing advertising. Our network-media buying takes place in New York—he pointed to one square in the grid, labeling it "New York"—while most spot buying takes place in Detroit. (Spot buying means purchasing time on local stations rather than network television.) He labeled a different square "Detroit." Creative executions for a number of different clients are produced in both of these full-service offices, New York and Detroit.

Next Pete pointed to one square in the grid, wrote "Atlanta" next to it, and said we had a big client in Atlanta that had its creative prepared in New York, and network media bought there. Most of the research for this client came out of Detroit, however, along with the spot buying and most of the print buying. Even though this client was very big ("maybe you've heard of it—diet Coke?") we didn't have an office in Atlanta—not even a field office.

He then pointed to another square in the grid, labeling it "Miami." This, Pete said, was where another big Lintas client was headquartered. In this case, the creative came mostly out of New York, although we switched it off frequently with the creative staff in Detroit. Our Miami client, Eastern Airlines, had an annual budget of some $100 million, almost all of it in fast-breaking retail advertising.

Everyone knew that airline advertising was much more fast-paced than the cruise business. The Eastern account, because of its size and the nature of the airline business, was clearly more difficult to manage than the Princess account would be.

We had a field office in Miami, Pete said, not a full-service office. We felt we needed a field office there to coordinate Eastern's heavy retail schedule properly.

Likewise, we planned to have a field office in Los Angeles (at this point Pete wrote "L.A." in one of the squares), to make sure we could coordinate Princess's retail activity, the same way we'd been coordinating Sitmar's activity with our L.A. field office for several years now. We'd probably expand it somewhat, but we'd still be buying print media and generating the creative product out of Detroit, while buying most of the broadcast media in New York.

Our other big L.A. client—Carnation—didn't *want* us to do creative and buy media from Los Angeles because, Pete said, their feeling was that the New York and Detroit offices made many more resources available to them than they could ever get from the biggest agency in Los Angeles.

All in all, it was a persuasive case. Pete delivered this entire message in less than five minutes, in his sunny, matter-of-fact manner. When he got to the end, he turned and smiled directly at Princess's CEO, sitting in the middle of the table between several other Princess executives.

"We think it's in your interest for us to manage your advertising this way," he said, "similar to the way we manage Eastern Airlines, Coke, and our other blue chip clients. This is the way we've always managed Sitmar's business. But before we spend another two hours making the rest of our presentation today, I want to make sure you agree that this makes sense."

Then Pete asked, "Is this okay?"

He stopped talking and waited for the CEO to give his answer.

When the CEO spoke, it was almost with a shrug. Okay, he said, he guessed that made sense. Tension left the room with a nearly audible sigh.

They were now capable of hearing what we had to say. We were free to win (or lose) the business on the strength of our thinking and presentation.

This time we won.

Unveiling Objections

Before we could chart a strategy to win the Princess account, we first had to determine what the CEO's objections might be. In this case, we learned about it from our own client-services people, who worked closely with junior and senior people in Princess's advertising and marketing departments.

But often it's not so easy. If you don't have ready access to information about the prospect and his potential objections to your pitch, the simplest approach is the direct one: ask. (For some guidance on how to sharpen your probe, see "Q & A," page 71.)

In many cases—more than you would probably guess—a prospective client won't really be in touch with the reasoning behind his own firm's decision. Sometimes that's because the decision was made over a period of days or weeks by a committee whose members don't all agree anyway. Sometimes it's because the issues involved in the decision are taken for granted to such an extent that they're all but invisible to the firm's executives. Often it's because there is some set of issues that a prospect finds just too painful or too difficult to think about objectively.

These are the areas you need to probe—issues taken for granted, or controversies too difficult to discuss openly.

Because the prospect company is probably making decisions by committee, and because different managers at the company are likely to hold contrary opinions, don't be satisfied with one executive's answers to these questions. Ask a number of different people at the prospect company. Ask the same person more than once. Get to the bottom of it several times. Compare notes with the other members of your pitch team.

Don't limit your questioning to the executives involved in the selection process. You can get a good feeling for the answers to these questions from a wide variety of executives who are there now, or who were recently employed there.

If your prospect has some overriding reason not to give you the business, like the CEO of Princess had regarding Lintas, you probably won't be able to overcome this obstacle simply by talking. At some point you have to get his actual agreement. You have to engage his participation in the process.

Overcoming a key objection requires you to lead the prospect in a process of joint discovery. Your prospect must be required to solve this problem, or to think about it in such a way that he "discovers" on his own that the obstacle is not an obstacle after all. Only by compelling your prospective client to participate intellectually in the process will you be able to win his business.

Q & A

Picture this: It's you and four other firms competing for an account, and the presentation is four weeks away. What do you have to know in order to sharpen your pitch? Everything you can find out, that's what. So get on the phone, call the prospect up, and ask him everything:

- *Why is his company changing agencies (or law firms, or software vendors, or architects, etc.)?*
- *What did he like about his former vendor? What did he most want to change?*
- *Who at his company made the final decision to fire the other vendor? Who started the ball rolling? Anybody try to stop it? Who and why?*
- *Who at his company put the list of competing vendors together? Why did they put our firm on the list? What about the others?*
- *What's the biggest reason he can think of not to give us the business?*

- *What's the biggest negative he thinks anyone else on the selection team would have with respect to our firm? What's the biggest positive?*

Overcoming the Final Objection: Money

Occasionally an objection will crop up at the end of an otherwise successful pitch, and it almost always has to do with money.

The *first* thing to do in any price negotiation is to shift the discussion from cost to value. When a prospect or client raises an objection as to cost, your first negotiating principle ought to be to add services to the offering.

"Gee, I know our prices aren't cheap, but what if we also were to . . . ?"

In the end, however, if money is a sticking point, then one of my favorite pitch tactics is the money-back guarantee.

I won a consulting assignment for myself from a large direct-marketing ad agency by using this tactic. I was going to charge a fairly high monthly retainer and I didn't want to negotiate my price. I was confident the head of this firm would appreciate the value I'd be able to give him for this retainer, but he wasn't so sure.

So I told him if he wasn't happy after the first sixty days, I'd give him his entire fee back. Every nickel. He agreed to do it on that basis and we had a very happy relationship for nearly two years.

My consulting firm won business from Pitney Bowes, a company that makes, sells, and leases postage meters and other mailing equipment, in exactly the same way. PB wanted to rethink their customer strategies. They were very intrigued with the philosophy of individualized marketing that Martha Rogers and I had written about in our book *The One to One Future: Building Relationships One Customer at a Time,* so they called my firm, *marketing 1:1,* and asked us to make a proposal.

Many of the strategies that we cover in our book are strategies that direct marketing firms are very familiar with. In direct mail, which is an addressable medium, it pays to treat customers individually and remember their past preferences, which basically was the philosophy we were advocating for the age of computers and electronically interactive marketing.

We learned that PB also asked for a proposal

Don Peppers

from Wunderman, one of the world's largest direct mail ad agencies. Now, if you're a direct mail ad agency, the way you make most of your money is by marking up the cost of producing and mailing millions of dollars worth of mailing pieces. That's where the real upside is. These firms are willing to give away consulting services in order to get those big-ticket production jobs.

Our proposal had a six-figure consulting fee attached, for a project that would take maybe three or four months. We knew Wunderman would propose no fee at all because they expected to have the direct mail campaign to pay off their costs. But even though Pitney Bowes is in the metered mail business, it wasn't at all clear that it needed a direct mail campaign. In fact it was very clear that what PB really needed was an entire rethinking of their customer-management and product-management processes.

So in our final meeting with PB, the question of money came up. "Well, gee, you guys are charging a very big fee here, and I got to tell you, your competitor isn't charging anything. He's going to do this for free because he wants business down the road."

Our answer was this: "If the only tool you have is

a hammer, then every problem looks like a nail. You can be fairly confident that whatever problems PB has, the solutions proposed by Wunderman will all involve heavy direct mailing. We might propose direct mail also, even though we don't execute it or create it. But if we do, it will be only because we have determined it's the most effective solution to your problem."

As persuasive as that argument was, what finally closed the deal was our money-back guarantee: Sign us up for one month's retainer, some $30,000. We'll invoice you now, and you'll pay us now. At the end of the month we'll have an evaluation meeting. If you're not satisfied that we delivered every nickel of that value and more, we'll give you your check back. We won't even cash it. We'll give it back to you right there. So at the end of the month we're going to give you either a check or an invoice for the next month.

Our consulting relationship with Pitney Bowes endured for more than a year.

Don Peppers

Using the Money-Back Guarantee to Land a Job

Many times, young people come to me and ask, "How am I going to break into advertising?" That's been my field, but I would give them the same advice whether they were trying to break into accounting or law or architecture or anything else.

What I tell them is this: First find a company you want to work for by identifying the business, culture, and people you'd be most comfortable with. Then go talk to the person who would hire you (not the personnel department), and tell him you'll work for the first month free. Totally free. You'll be there full-time, and it will cost them nothing. All you want is a chance to demonstrate what you can do for the company.

Tell them if they take you up on this offer, they have to keep you there for a full thirty days. Sign confidentiality agreements and everything, so you'll really be an employee. They can pay you a dollar a week, or something like that.

At the end of that thirty-day period, if you haven't proved that you're an employee worth keeping at a reasonable salary, you'll leave. But if you have proved it, then they'll pay you the salary for that thirty days, and they'll hire you.

All you have to do is get the interview, and then make that kind of an offer. Just making the offer is going to be enough to get somebody's attention.

Chapter 8
▼▼▼▼▼▼

Stop. Look. LISTEN

 Listen to your prospects for key words. Then speak their language.

When I was at Levine, Huntley, one of my cold calls reached John, the marketing director at Friendly Ice Cream, which was at that time owned by Hershey. Even though John expressed no dissatisfaction with his current agency, I kept in touch with him, periodically sending along a news clipping, or calling to discuss something I thought he might find interesting.

I took careful notes during the three or four telephone conversations we had over the two years following my *initial call to him. I noted John's use of certain key words to describe Friendly's corporate culture. The best kind of management, he had said, was "delegate, delegate, delegate." Friendly's CEO and all the senior executives had bought into the philosophy of "management by empowerment." Managers were expected to "rise to the challenge."*

Two years later, when we were invited to pitch for Friendly's business, these key phrases helped us formulate a winning strategy.

▼▼▼▼▼▼▼

Friendly announced that every day for thirteen straight business days the company would hear a different agency make its two-hour initial presentation in the company's conference room in Framingham, Massachusetts. Their "short list" was pretty long. The sessions were all scheduled from five-thirty P.M. to seven-thirty P.M., so they could be attended not only by the marketing staff, but by the finance director, the production manager, the CEO, and an assortment of other senior managers.

Levine, Huntley drew the twelfth position, which we considered an excellent spot for distinguishing ourselves from the agencies that were to precede us. We came up with a strategy for proving that we spoke Friendly's language, while at the same time showing how different we

Don Peppers

were from the other agencies in the competition. (Had we drawn a different position, we would have used an entirely different strategy.)

Our basic presentation involved a quick description of our own firm, along with some "case studies" showing our work for other clients and the results of that advertising. Then we presented a synopsis of our view of the sit-down restaurant business, Friendly's position within that category, and a strategy for improving it. This was all standard stuff, but it was what Friendly had asked for, and every agency had to show they could do it.

We knew all our competitors would bring their president or chairman. Even an agency thirty times our size, like Saatchi & Saatchi, would probably bring its North American CEO. Three of the four partners who formed Levine, Huntley, Schmidt and Beaver were still active in the business on a daily basis (the fourth, retired newsman Chet Huntley, had died shortly after the agency was founded). But regardless of their availability for the meeting, we elected not to bring any of our partners to it. There were no "names on the door" at our presentation.

Sure enough, about halfway through our pitch, John asked us the question we had been expecting. He leaned forward over the table and remarked that yesterday Marvin Sloves, the top dog at Scali, McCabe, Sloves, had led his agency's pitch. Ed Wax, the CEO of Saatchi & Saatchi,

had been there a few days ago. Jack Connors, the chairman of Hill, Holliday, Connors, Cosmopulos, had re-
arranged his schedule, canceling a trip to the West Coast
just so he could be there for the meeting with Friendly.
But none of our partners had been able to attend? He
didn't say it, but he was implying our partners might have
better things to do than try to prove to Friendly how
much we wanted their business.

Our response appeared totally spontaneous, although
every word had been carefully weighed during the pitch
rehearsal. We are an agency that believes in "management
by empowerment." We push responsibility as far down in
the organization as we can, so the people you see are the
people who will actually do the work on your account.
Our agency's philosophy is "delegate, delegate, delegate."
Our belief is that if we delegate responsibility and em-
power people, they will "rise to the challenge."

Immediately, everybody in the Friendly audience sat
up, looked around, and brightened. We were like them.
We understood. Our ideas on the sit-down restaurant
business suddenly seemed smarter to them, more thought
out. Our advertising creativity was fresher, brighter. They
began to listen more carefully to what we had to say.

Friendly had a final round which involved us and one
other agency, and then they gave us their account.

Did we trick Friendly into something that was not in

their own interest? Not at all. Our agency really was a "delegate, delegate, delegate" kind of place. We simply formulated a strategy that would emphasize our bond with them.

We didn't just listen to them to prepare for our pitch. During our presentation we spoke their language.

Chapter 9

▼▼▼▼▼▼

Become the Customer

 What you say and what your prospect hears may be two different things—sometimes very different.

The human mind attempts to fit each new piece of information into an integrated, consistent whole. After a lifetime of looking, listening, and absorbing information, each of us expects certain facts to follow others. Information that doesn't fit with our expectations is often filtered out.

That's why it's so important to identify with your prospect. If you don't understand her point of view, which is influenced not only by past experience and expectations for the future, but by her own psychological needs, you may have a great deal of trouble communicating with her. She may filter out half of what you say, making it impossible for you to get your message across.

Penetrating Corporate Culture

To win a pitch you have to be able to identify with the prospect firm's *belief system* and sculpt your presentation accordingly. Try to understand what view of reality dominates the company's culture. To understand a company's belief system, you must know the answers to the following questions:

How like-minded are the managers at your prospect's company?

Do most of the managers at the prospect's company seem to view reality the same way?

If so, what do they value? What do they fear? What do they rally around?

If not, how diverse are the views inside the company? Are there large differences among departments or subsidiaries? Are there generational differences? Which generation is in charge of the pitch decision?

What is the company's approach to problem-solving?

Can you get a clear picture of problem-solving as it would take place at the prospect's company?

Is this the way you solve your own company's problems?

Could you visualize your business if it solved problems this way?

What rewards and penalties are given to managers?

If you were an executive at the prospect company, what kind of accomplishment would benefit your career?

How fast could you rise at this company?

Is it easy to fail? Does the company tolerate failure?

How self-aware is the company?

Does it appear to be an introspective organization?

Do managers spend time going over their own issues, investing frequently in training and off-site workshops?

Or is the organization driven by the constant pressure of outside events?

Do they ever have time to take a breath and look more carefully at the long-term situation?

What is the firm's decision-making process?

How does the company actually make its choices?

How does it decide on particular issues or policies?

Is the process predicated on consensus-building?

Does every organizational subgroup have to buy off on important issues?

Or does the company appear to be driven more by "intra-preneurship" and individual initiative?

Does the company celebrate any internal heroes?

Does the company have legends?

What is the company's overall approach to management and organizational structure?

How much delegation of responsibility and authority exists within the company?

Is authority concentrated more at the top, or do middle- and junior-level executives make important policy decisions?

How does the senior management treat the middle management?

What perks do the senior managers enjoy? How deferential are their subordinates?

A company's belief system may be obvious once you understand the company's industry or business itself. Highly competitive retailing organizations like Princess Cruises and Circuit City are likely to have an entirely different culture than larger, slower, packaged-goods companies like Carnation. But even within similar industries, different competitors almost certainly will have totally different corporate cultures. Over the past decade I've worked, at different times, as a consultant for AT&T and MCI, for instance. AT&T, a deliberate, introspective organization, aims for incremental, carefully planned improvement. The younger, smaller MCI, in contrast, is more impulsive, and shoots for significant results over a shorter time frame. Most MCI marketing executives are totally uninterested in any program that doesn't have "network news" potential. Just as dissimilar are Toyota and Isuzu. Or Chase Manhattan and Citicorp.

Once you're confident you understand at least something about your prospect's corporate culture, try to determine how closely your own firm identifies with that culture. Chances are, even if your company's culture is not very similar to your prospect's, there will be at least one or two common threads. Any area of cultural similarity could prove to be a useful tool in the pitch.

Remember: In every pitch situation, a prospect will be looking at several organizations, most staffed with total strangers. If you want to win a pitch, you have to give the prospect some basis for identifying with the staff members in your firm. The prospect must *want* to get to know you.

A Tale of Two Friends

Two former IBM sales representatives are now married to each other. Alan was voted most likely to succeed by his class of IBM sales trainees, while Mary, believe it or not, was voted least likely to succeed by her class. Alan did okay. But Mary did sensationally.

Mary became the hottest IBM sales rep in New York and at one point in her career was designated the best IBM sales rep in the entire nation. She would gobble up prospects and convert them to sales, yet she did everything unconventionally. She didn't sell by the book. Selling was never a by-the-numbers exercise for Mary.

Instead, she would concentrate on putting herself in the shoes of the customer. She would think about things from the customer's perspective, concentrating on learning the customer's worldview. She would *become* the customer.

Alan accompanied Mary on her sales calls one day, just to see what her secret was, and he says she wore him out. Her technique was different at each call. But she closed a sale at nearly every meeting she attended.

If a client was worried about cost, a typical conversation would go like this: The customer might say, "What do you think about this machine here, or this piece of system architecture?" And Mary would reply, "Oh, no, that's way too expensive for you. You don't need to do that. You want to stick with this less-expensive system." Then the customer would start arguing, insisting that he needed a higher capability. She'd say, "No, you could get this lower-cost machine first and then move up." But eventually the customer would insist on buying the bigger system, the higher-priced piece of equipment.

Mary's technique was to work from the inside, from an understanding of the customer's desire to save money, rather than trying to beat down resistance to paying more for a larger system.

Mary's customers felt she was more concerned with their balance sheet than with her sales quotas. As a result, they had no hesitation about giving her their business.

Chapter 10

▼▼▼▼▼▼

Make Me Rich, Make Me Famous

Belelieve it or not, most people fall into one of two personality types: "make me rich" and "make me famous." I use this typecasting as an aid in deciding what sort of argument is most likely to succeed with the person on the other end of the conversation.

A make-me-rich person is a no-nonsense, get-to-the-bottom-line conversationalist. He or she is often economical with words, doesn't like long letters or memos, and hates long conversations even more. Everything a make-me-rich executive does is measured and prioritized on the basis of its effect on his objective, which is usually tangible and quantifiable.

Make-me-rich people have what I call "bottom-line disease." They are obsessed with results and outcomes. Terms such as *deliverables, action items,* and *benchmarks* characterize their vocabulary. A sure sign of bottom-line disease is a premature desire to close the conversation— to get to the conclusion, wrap it up, nail it down. Now. Let's do it.

No matter how interesting or compelling your case might be, if you can't put it in twenty-five words for a make-me-rich person, you'll lose his attention. Period. He'll just tune out, think about something else, and you'll probably never get him back.

The make-me-rich executive usually has a very strong personality and quickly gets his way in any large organization. If a marketing department is headed by such a person, for example, you'll find everyone in the department using the same results-oriented vocabulary he uses, and many will exhibit the same basic impatience.

Hint: Just because a person talks about getting results doesn't mean he's obsessed, and may not indicate a make-me-rich mentality. But it does indicate the nearby presence and strong influence of this personality type—probably at a more senior level.

Don Peppers

At the other end of this scale is the make-me-famous person. He wants to be admired. He likes to entertain. He may be just as busy and impatient as the make-me-rich person, but he'll go for a punch line instead of the bottom line anyway. He'll tell you a story or relate a humorous anecdote whenever he gets the chance.

The make-me-famous executive may define success the same way a make-me-rich executive does, but his measurement process includes an extra step. He wants results, but he wants others to see the results too.

The make-me-rich executive asks: "What effect will this have on the bottom line?"

The make-me-famous executive asks the same question this way: "What will others think of the effect this has on the bottom line?"

To a make-me-famous executive, a tree falling in the woods makes no sound if no one is around to hear it. In his worldview, the only proof of his existence is the effect he has on others.

Bringing Home Clues from the Office

When I have an opportunity to visit with a prospect, the one thing I like to do best is meet him in his own office. You can get a lot of interesting and useful insight into a prospect's personality simply by taking a look around at how the office is decorated, how it gets set up for meetings, and how it's stocked with equipment and books.

A make-me-rich person will often make his office into a spare, utilitarian workspace. The wall might be hung with art, but it will be company-issue and unremarkable. The art won't be hung to generate comment, but to avoid drabness. Have you ever walked into a senior executive's office and been shocked by how sparse the furniture is, or how cluttered with papers and files the desk surface is? Chances are, the occupant of that office belongs to the make-me-rich category.

Bookshelves in a make-me-rich office will be stocked to overflowing with reference books and manuals, and often with business how-to books. Look first for novels, cartoons, or art books—anything unrelated to business. If you don't find any, you are in a make-me-rich office.

If there's a table in the office, the make-me-rich executive will use it. It won't be for show. This is where meetings will be conducted, in easy reach of the rest of his office, his phone, computer, secretary, and so forth. Often, even a very senior executive with a beautiful high-floor office will have his own conference table piled high with research documents or work papers. He may treat the table as simply another source of desk surface area.

The make-me-famous person, on the other hand, will put a lot of effort into his visible status, and this will be quite noticeable in his office. He'll put awards and photographs on the wall, along with carefully chosen—and unique—artwork. On his desk, more than likely, will be photographs of family and friends, showing boating excursions or picnics together, or a school play, or just a family group shot. Any time you go into an office and have the impression that the office is clean, spotless, or arranged "just so"—that office belongs to a make-me-famous type.

The make-me-famous person even dresses a little more elegantly—if you find cuff links or monograms, you're hot on the trail.

A make-me-famous person accepts compliments, flattery, and praise with no pangs of embarrassment. But compliment a make-me-rich person and he'll fidget, then turn the conversation to the factual results of the program —numbers, sales, statistics.

While the division between these two personality types may seem simple, it's not always obvious. Here's a quick exercise to help you practice recognizing different personality types:

Walk into an office you've never been in before, look around, and classify the occupant into the "rich" or "famous" category. Then pay attention to the way he or she holds a conversation with you to see if you were right. If all else fails, and the situation isn't awkward, ask this question:

"If you could only be (a) rich, or (b) famous, but not both, which would you choose?"

Caviar and Carnegie Hall: Courting a Make-Me-Famous Personality

I once spent a long time trying to get in to see Dave, a new executive at Pepsi. Dave had just been assigned to Pepsi after overseeing the advertising at Pizza Hut, a Pepsico company. He was now second in command to Alan Pottasch, the man who had been in charge of Pepsi's advertising for as long as anyone could remember.

So far I had had no luck at all in making contact

with Pottasch, who was an industry legend. But Alan was due to retire any year now, and Pepsi was trying to find a worthy successor. Dave was not the first candidate who had been given a shot at it.

In any case, I figured if I could get in to see Dave, then Levine, Huntley might have a chance at landing some assignments from Pepsi. We had no thought of winning the main brand. But this was a very large company, and it had all sorts of little brands, new products, and advertising projects that could make our agency quite happy.

We were a hot agency, but no matter what I did, I couldn't get Dave to return my calls. I called and I called. I sent him a letter. Then another. There was absolutely no sign of interest.

With all this effort, however, I had become very good friends with his secretary. So I asked her about Dave in order to try to learn something about him. "What does your boss do in his spare time?" I asked her. "What's he like as a boss?"

I also asked her what kinds of pictures he had in his new office. "What things did he bring from the Pizza Hut job?"

She said he had lots of pictures and souvenirs from various commercial shoots he had attended while supervising the advertising at Pizza Hut—a company that had done some pretty clever advertising at some point. To shoot these commercials, Pizza Hut had used a very well-known director. The secretary said that Dave had a couple of pictures on his bookshelf and desk that showed him with this director, and in one shot he was pictured with the president of Pizza Hut's advertising agency.

Bingo! A make-me-famous personality if there ever was one! Obviously, Dave wanted to be recognized. He wanted to be seen.

"Does Dave like to go out at all?" I asked his secretary. But of course I already knew the answer to that.

"Oh, yes," she said. She told me he particularly liked being assigned to the New York area, after his long stint in Wichita, Pizza Hut's hometown. She said he knew a number of New York restaurants, and was happy to be near them regularly, instead of just on business trips.

"Well, my wife and I have four tickets to a Carnegie Hall concert two weeks from today," I told his secretary. "Afterward, we'd like to go to Petrossian for a bite. Why don't you ask Dave if he and his wife would like to join us?" I added that my wife, Pamela, was a TV producer in business on her own.

Petrossian, as I figured Dave would know, is one of the most expensive and glittery restaurants in the city. It was beyond trendy. Just a block from Carnegie Hall, Petrossian specialized in caviar, foie gras, champagne, and old money.

Half an hour later I got a call back from his secretary. Invitation accepted. Just like that. I'd never even spoken to this guy on the phone, and he agreed to a whole evening out on the town, wives and all.

So why did I get through to him with an invitation rather than with calls and business letters? Because I appealed to what he was most interested in. He wanted to be liked, to be entertained, to be seen. Straightforward appeals that were strictly business did not speak to this make-me-famous personality.

We went to Carnegie Hall and dined at Petrossian. The four of us had a dinner tab alone of more than a thousand dollars.

When my boss saw the bill on my expense account, he hit the roof. I countered that Dave was the kind of guy who had to be wined and dined. And from the conversation that night I had become convinced that further investment in his entertainment would not be unwise.

Sure enough, within four months we were invited to participate in a review for one of Pepsi's new products.

How to Handle the Rich or Famous

When you're preparing for a pitch, keep these rules in mind:

1. If you're calling or meeting someone you've never met before, then have on the tip of your tongue a very quick, right-to-the-point statement about why you're calling, what you want, when, and how. The very instant you realize you're dealing with a make-me-rich person, drop any ancillary discussion and get right to it. Lead with your conclusions.

2. Don't even try to take a make-me-rich person out to a play, concert, or sporting event. And business lunches had better be all business too.

3. If you're dealing with a make-me-famous person, take time to entertain and be entertained. If

you have friends in common, be sure to work on them—he will probably consult them for their judgments.

4. The most persuasive words you can use to a make-me-famous person are: "No one has ever done this before. This will put your company on the map."

Chapter 11

▼▼▼▼▼▼

Changing the Rules

 If you want to win, you've got to do more than sell your brilliant ideas and psychoanalyze your prospect. You've got to out-maneuver your competitors.

inning demands competitive thinking. Here are two simple strategic principles that should help you gain the advantage in almost any pitch situation:

1. Look for *all* the differences between you and your competitors—not just what you do better, but what they do poorly. Make the most of those differences.

Don Peppers

2. Watch for opportunities to change the rules. Any time you can convince your prospect to make a change that will hurt your competition more than it hurts you—do it.

The following are two instances when my colleagues and I used these principles to our advantage:

Making Time at MCI

When my agency was competing for the $50 million MCI business, we were up against four much larger companies and stress-inducing deadlines. (The pitch started in mid-August, and MCI wanted to hire a new agency *and* have the new ad campaign ready to air in November!)

We had five weeks to turn the project around, but I figured that a tight deadline imposed a much more difficult burden on our four large competitors, each of which was less flexible and more laden with demanding assignments from big clients.

Rather than trying to get as much time as possible to do the best job we could, we suggested the opposite. After checking with our creative director and determining that we could bring on enough freelance talent to get the assignment completed, I told MCI that we would be prepared to present recommendations in ten days—an entire month earlier than they asked—provided that MCI could get each of the other agencies to agree to the same deadline. This way, I argued, MCI would have more time to make its final decision.

It worked. MCI took us up on our offer. After hearing presentations from all five agencies, they eliminated three, inviting our agency and Wells Rich Greene to present additional ideas two weeks later, about the same time as the original deadline.

By changing the rules, we had handicapped our competitors and improved our own odds.

Friendly Competition

Immediately following the presentation to Friendly, in which we demonstrated our understanding of the company's "delegate, delegate, delegate" corporate culture, the marketing vice president took me aside to ask for advice on conducting the rest of the review. The thirteenth and last of his semifinal agency presentations was to occur the day after ours, and as he walked me to the door after our meeting, he took me aside and said that

Don Peppers

while the decision was not final, it was likely that we would be competing for his account in the final round. His question was "How should I structure the final round to make the best decision?"

This was an unusual request, to say the least. I had no way of knowing if he had asked any of the other agencies this same question, but my guess was that he certainly had not asked many. I later found out he hadn't asked anyone else at all.

It was an ideal situation for us because, if Friendly followed our advice, we could change the rules of engagement for our competitors. We had two goals in responding to Friendly's request:

First, we needed to suggest a structure for the final round that would appeal to them and reflect our insight into Friendly's culture.

Second, we had a competitive opportunity to handicap our rivals by rearranging the playing field.

One limitation was that we had no idea who our competitors would be in the final round. We knew, approximately, the slate of thirteen semifinal agencies, but we didn't know which ones Friendly liked besides us. We asked them, but we didn't expect them to tell us, and they wouldn't.

We wanted the best possible odds for ourselves, and that would mean the fewest possible competitors. So, our next goal was to design a format that would make it all but impossible for Friendly to accommodate more than one or two other agencies. We had to design a time-consuming, grueling final round.

At that time the traditional format for the last-round advertising agency competition was a set of two-hour presentations from each of the half-dozen or so finalists. What we proposed to Friendly was totally different: a "think-off" between two or, at most, three agencies. We advised Friendly to visit each finalist agency's office for an entire day of impromptu discussions with the executives who would be assigned to their account.

What we meant by impromptu was that the account team and creative staff would join Friendly in the agency conference room, where the restaurant company's executives would pose some previously undisclosed problem from the sit-down restaurant category. Without time to prepare an answer in advance, the agency staff members would be left to their own wits.

We told Friendly it was important to change the problem from one agency to the next—radically—because every agency was an information sieve, and if the same problem were posed to each agency, then it would be a truly impromptu discussion only at the first office.

Following a morning of discussion designed to identify how an agency really thought about its business, we sug-

$\mathcal{D}on\ \mathcal{P}eppers$

gested that Friendly executives use the afternoon to meet, individually, with the media planners, creative teams, and account executives who would be spending half or more of their time on the Friendly business. These meetings should exclude senior agency people entirely!

As far as any of us knew, no one had ever structured a final-round agency competition this way. If Friendly accepted our advice, we knew this structure would have several advantages for us. First, because of the all-day format, Friendly simply would not be able to accommodate more than two or three agencies in the final round. It would require too much of their executives' time to visit more than three agencies. We thought they'd probably try to hold it to two, if they could—and we already knew we'd be one of them.

Second, particularly because of the individual meetings we recommended in the afternoon, we thought the structure would appeal to Friendly's sense of how corporations ought to be managed. Friendly would want an agency that trusted its middle managers to carry the ball, and we wanted to emphasize our understanding of this aspect of their corporate culture.

Third, we knew that any agency entering the final round with us would be totally unaccustomed to this kind of competition. We wanted a final-round format that left our competitors scratching their heads in bewilderment.

Without question, this kind of final competition would impose a heavy burden on our agency. It would require more preparation, and more commitment of resources in advance of winning the account. But we knew that when sprung as a surprise, it would impose a much more difficult burden on our competitors, no matter who they were.

The structure we suggested to Friendly was not intended to make the final round simpler or easier for ourselves, but to improve our relative position. And it was one of the keys to our winning the business.

Chapter 12

▼▼▼▼▼▼▼

Sleuthing to Win

Preparing for a pitch is a lot like doing police work. You've got to check sources, corroborate stories, scour for clues.

Like any detective approaching a new case, your first step should be to learn everything about a prospect that is publicly known. Next, to the extent possible, you should ask the prospect directly whatever it is you need to know: What's the company's corporate culture? Who's making the decisions about the pitch? On what basis? If you do a good job gathering information, you will probably arrive at the starting gate about as well informed as your competitors.

However, if you come armed with *intelligence*—useful information that is not public—you will have a leg up.

Rumors, Innuendo, and the Trade Press

One great source of advance, nonpublic information is the trade press. I'm not talking about reading articles in trade magazines, although that certainly helps. I'm talking about developing useful relationships with the reporters who write the articles. Nonpublic information is the "currency" that drives this kind of relationship.

My method for cultivating relationships will work with reporters who cover any beat. But it works especially well in advertising, one of the most self-absorbed industries anyone could imagine.

To a trade press reporter, getting the scoop on an advertising review not yet public is the stuff journalism is made of. And for a rainmaker, learning of a not-yet-public advertising review makes the heart beat faster. In other words, trade press reporters and business-development executives share a common interest in obtaining nonpublic information before it becomes "news."

My philosophy about reporters is the same as my philosophy about search consultants: It can never hurt to have a friendly relationship. I will go out of my way to put a reporter in my debt, if possible—and it's often possible.

Before you pick up the phone to talk to a trade press reporter, comb through a couple of back issues of his magazine or trade paper and note a few of the articles with his byline. There are two reasons for doing this. First, you want to know what the reporter has been working on recently, the angle he's taken, and the type of reporting he does. Second, reporters like to be read. It's always a good idea to throw a comment into your conversation indicating you've read a story he wrote.

No advertising agency can participate in every review it is offered. Frequently agencies turn down the opportunity to compete because of a conflict with other business —maybe the review is for an airline account, and you already have one airline client or your subsidiary does the direct marketing or sales promotion for one of the airline's competitors. Or maybe you know you can't possibly win the business, so you elect not to compete. Or maybe you'd like to pitch an account but you're already tied up in four other pending competitions and can't spare the staff. Or perhaps the account just isn't big enough to go after.

Far from being a wasted asset, every declined pitch is an opportunity to trade intelligence with a reporter, or with a colleague at another agency. I like nothing better than calling a reporter and letting him in on the fact that a review is planned and no one else knows about it. If I were planning on pitching for the account myself, I wouldn't dream of blabbing the news to a reporter, who will write a story alerting all my competitors. But since I'm not pitching, I can at least do a favor for someone who, eventually, is likely to do a favor for me.

It's pointless to keep score very accurately, but after you tip off a few different reporters, you'll soon learn which ones know how to return the favor. They're the ones who, when they're working on a story about an upcoming review, will call you and ask for your comments, or for what you know. You probably know nothing, and they may know you know nothing, but they want to continue to receive scoops like the one or two you've given them in the past.

Having better intelligence than your competitors is always beneficial. Sometimes it's indispensable. Doing favors for members of one of the only professions with lower public esteem than advertising people is a small price to pay.

Don Peppers

Using the Trade Press to Foul Up Competitors

My favorite tactic for damaging a competitor's prospects is to plant a rumor in the trade press that his firm has a lock on the account. I also try to work in a mention that my firm is a long shot. I would never be quoted in a story like this, but I might spread the rumor off the record. Or I would call a friend and ask him to call the reporter.

Nothing makes the people conducting the review more uncomfortable than giving the impression that the review process is anything but completely fair and rational. A story about a leading candidate, therefore, often damages that candidate's chances and boosts the chances of his competitors. When I was at Lintas we got involved in a pitch competition that was being run by a search consultant who had very significant personal relationships with the executives at one of the agencies participating. (The agency CEO was actually the consultant's best friend. Their families vacationed together. The CEO had once found the consultant another job after the consultant had been let go when his employer was taken over.)

Now, there's certainly nothing wrong with having personal friendships such as this, but we suspected the consultant had not told his client how special his relationship with this particular agency was. We wanted the prospect to know the truth, so any recommendations by the consultant would be objectively appraised.

Our solution was to ensure that this news made its way to a trade press reporter. I didn't, however, simply call the reporter myself. We wanted to neutralize our competitor's advantage, but we didn't want to be seen as squealers. So I prevailed on a close friend at another agency, uninvolved in this particular competition, to call the reporter who was covering this pitch and give her the details.

Using Intelligence Strategically

Nonpublic information can do a lot more than just tip you off about a pitch in advance of your competitors. It can provide leverage for actually winning a pitch.

My favorite use for nonpublic information about a prospective client is what I call the "telepathic" pitch. Telepathy, in my definition, involves providing information to a prospect that is so insightful, so prescient, so in synch with the prospect's own point of view that it appears telepathic.

I once discovered, for instance, that my agency was

locked out of an important pitch—for Skippy peanut butter's U.S. advertising account. Lintas was an ideal agency for this kind of packaged-goods client—we had no conflicts, and we were just across the Hudson River from CPC/Best Foods' New Jersey headquarters, where the Skippy brand was managed. But the review had been publicly announced without our hearing about it in advance. Best Foods had put its list of agencies together, and we weren't on it. I couldn't get the marketing director to return my calls, nor was she likely to.

In a desperate effort to get some kind of information about the review, I canvassed our worldwide network of agencies for anyone who might have a contact with Best Foods. Canada yielded a surprising benefit.

The previous year, Lintas had acquired a large, independent Canadian advertising agency, MacLaren. MacLaren, it turned out, handled the Skippy brand in Canada. One way to get introduced to the Skippy people would be to use the MacLaren relationship.

However, the problem with this approach, I've found, is that even though you're dealing with the same company, when you begin approaching different people in different departments of the company you often encounter a "not invented here" philosophy that hinders your progress. Occasionally it can even be counterproductive to get your introduction this way.

But when I talked with the account executive in Toronto who handled the Skippy business, he said he had recently been to New Jersey, and he'd been given the text of the U.S. organization's confidential marketing plan. So I asked for a copy.

Why not? Our agency offices were owned by the same company, and we did not handle any of Skippy's competitors. Moreover, I verified that the confidentiality agreement MacLaren had signed with their client specifically allowed sharing such information with affiliated companies. Truth is, very little in most marketing plans can really be classified as brilliant, insightful, or competitively devastating. Of the dozens of marketing plans I've written, approved, read, or reviewed during my career, the only ones that ever seemed to warrant extreme secrecy were those two or three that revealed truly new products or services still in the planning stage. Most of the others, while often providing interesting perspectives, contained no genuinely precious information.

Best Foods' marketing plan for Skippy was no exception. On reviewing the plan, it was clear the company had three principal goals for the product in the coming years, but these goals would not have been difficult to derive just by sitting down and thinking hard about Skippy's current competitive situation, as shown from information that was publicly available. However, now I had information about the prospect's own thinking with regard to Skippy peanut butter over the next five years. It was nonpublic information that no one knew we had, so it was a perfect opportunity to take the telepathic approach.

I faxed a letter to the marketing director who was never available on the phone. In the letter I said that in our own analysis of Skippy's situation we felt the company should try to accomplish three things over the next few years, and I listed the three goals from the firm's own marketing plan. Naturally, I was careful to disguise the language and order of these goals, as well as the rationale that led to them.

I faxed this letter in the morning and in the afternoon I got a call from the marketing director inviting us to a meeting. She was impressed by our insight.

Finding and Using "Moles"

In nearly every winning pitch I've ever witnessed, a key role is played by a "mole." A mole is usually a person inside a prospect organization who is partial to your firm and who provides you with information designed to help you win the pitch. Moles can also be people who, though not employed by the prospect organization, are much more familiar with it, or with one of its key players, than you are.

The mole is the most valuable of all intelligence sources.

It was our mole, one very close to the Circuit City selection team, who let us know exactly what their plans were for the set of semifinal meetings, for instance. Without this information we wouldn't have had a chance of resurrecting our candidacy.

If you don't have a mole helping you with a particular pitch, remember that any serious competitor probably does. The winner will almost certainly rely on extremely good information from a knowledgeable, enthusiastic source.

How do you go about locating and cultivating a mole? Start with your own firm. If you've done your homework, you'll already know if any of your employees has a close relationship with any employees of the prospect organization. Any rainmaker who's been at it more than a month should already have a list of every manager's previous employers.

If one of your managers used to work at the prospect firm, approach her and ask for all the information she can remember, the names of senior executives she's on friendly terms with, the nature of the company's corporate culture, and the extent of her current contacts.

Don't forget spouses. Many professional employees are

married to other professionals who might have some affili-
ation with the firm you're trying to penetrate.

Be careful not to overstep the boundaries here. Get
from your own people whatever they feel comfortable
telling you, but don't push for anything that would put
them in the position of having to betray some trust or
confidence.

Other Sources of Moles

Never throw a résumé away.

Think about all the job applicants you or your personnel department have interviewed in the last few months
or years. It's likely that one or two of them worked at the
prospect company at some point in their past, perhaps
even close to the people in charge of the current review.
Or maybe one or two recent job applicants worked at the
prospect's current advertising agency. You never know
when it might be helpful to call a former job applicant in
for another interview.

Or, find the person inside the prospect organization
itself who wants to have an influence over events, who
believes that you're the right choice and that his colleagues, if left to their own devices, might not see this.
People disagree all the time, and someone inside the or-

ganization might want to give you an advantage, for reasons of his own.

Even a secretary or administrative assistant can give you a great deal of insight into the inner workings of a company. If you call the company frequently, you're apt to be on regular speaking terms with one of these phone gatekeepers sooner or later. Make it sooner.

Besides asking a secretary once in a while to tell me what her boss is like, I've asked administrative assistants to give me a quick summary of the company's management philosophy—delegation of responsibility, allocation of authority among management levels, and so forth. I once got a complete rundown on how the agency was selected last time around—from the person who typed the report, not the one who wrote it.

The point is, you don't have to bribe or blackmail to locate a mole who can help you win a pitch.

Why not find someone who simply likes you? Cultivate a friend.

Cleaning Up After Your Competitors

If you're lucky enough to win the contest for new business, the first thing you should do is offer to clean out your new client's office. "We'll take all this stuff cluttering your office and put it in storage, in case you ever need it." The "stuff" is the packages, videotapes, and brochures your competition sent to impress the client.

Most VPs, who are drowning in this material, will love your solution to their problem. And, of course, the material will give you terrific insight into your competitors' strengths, weaknesses, and strategies. You can read their pitch letters and study their case studies. It's a great way to gain competitive intelligence.

Sometimes you'll even get some prospecting ideas by reviewing a competitor's self-congratulatory descriptions of work done on current clients. (Remember that everything in a case study should be commercially nonsensitive or else the agency would not have released the information to a prospect.)

Once you've cleaned out two or three new clients' offices and compiled a file of your competitors' documents, you may find that, by coincidence, you have an opportunity to compete for business they've boasted about during a prior competition.

Chapter 13

▼▼▼▼▼▼

Stage Fright

$\int$ takes are high. The adrenaline is running. No wonder, the final pitch meeting is when business can be won or lost. But if you think you're the only one who's nervous, you've missed out on another opportunity to boost your odds.

 Your Prospect May Be More Scared Than You Are

I'll never forget my first encounter with the advertising agency world. A lowly marketing executive at Texas International Airlines in Houston, I was on my way in to see my boss, the marketing VP, when his secretary stopped me.

"You can't go in there," she whispered, motioning at my boss's closed door.

"There's a *creative* in there."

It was the first time I had ever heard the word used as a noun—meaning a professional writer, producer, or art director. This particular creative was down from our New York advertising agency, Scali, McCabe. He later emerged from my boss's office dressed in a white linen suit and Panama hat! This guy had no qualms at all about being different. He was a presence. I'd never seen anything like it before.

When I went to work at Levine, Huntley, one of the best creatives at the firm was also one of the most volcanic personalities I'd ever met. When you disagreed with him in an otherwise quiet meeting, he thought nothing of yelling and cursing inches from your face.

Even his *looks* were scary. With a thick black beard and long hair, Jay resembled a cross between a Brooklyn rabbi and an Arab terrorist. He had a terrific sense of humor, was a genuine genius when it came to writing advertising, and was paid more for his talents than all but a handful of top executives at any of our client companies—altogether, a highly intimidating person to be around.

Eventually I learned how to work alongside such geniuses without feeling overly inferior. But I never forgot that initial sense of awe.

Now, put yourself in the shoes of a prospect executive, making the rounds of two or three finalist advertising agencies or law firms in competition for his account. At each location he encounters more creatives, lawyers, architects, or other highly intelligent professionals proficient in a field he is totally unfamiliar with. They may be witty and irreverent. They are also likely to be quite good at public speaking, a skill most people shy away from.

In addition to being intimidated, a prospect executive's career may hinge on his decision to hire one agency over another. If he hires a firm that doesn't produce results, it may cost him his job. Who wouldn't be nervous?

Casting

If you're selling any kind of sophisticated service, figure at least one or two executives on the prospect's side of the table are going to be somewhat intimidated, both by your firm's professional talents and by the presentation skills of the people on your side.

Consequently, one of your first tasks in a pitch meeting

is to put these executives more at ease, and to give them people on your side they can identify with. You need to create a sense of connection between your prospect and your own people.

One way to do this is by "casting," choosing people for your presentation team who have something in common with the prospect executives who will attend the pitch. Send a woman if there is a woman on the review committee, send a younger staffer if there are younger executives, send a midwesterner if a committee member is from the Midwest, and so on. As much as possible, match each person on the committee with someone he or she can identify with. This will do a great deal to put the committee members at ease with your firm, which can only work in your favor.

Be careful to watch out for make-me-rich and make-me-famous personalities on the prospect's side of the table. A make-me-rich person not only won't relate to a make-me-famous personality, he'll likely be outright hostile.

If you know the prospect is dominated by a make-me-rich personality, it is absolutely essential to give this person a make-me-rich personality on your own side that he or she can talk to. If the CEO of your firm is a make-me-famous type (as many successful executives are), don't make the mistake of matching him with the prospect just because they're both CEOs.

The same argument doesn't apply in the other direction, however. A make-me-famous prospect can be put at ease by anyone who is friendly, interesting, and helpful. And while that might not be a natural state for most make-me-rich people, it can usually be achieved with conscious effort.

De-Slicking Your Presentation

Some presentations are so smoothly delivered by agency executives, they come off as slick, and a slick presentation rarely wins the account. I think this has to do with trust and credibility. When you listen to a slick, flawless presentation, you can easily find yourself thinking, "These guys could sell ice to Eskimos." Facing a glib, smooth, polished speaker is not only intimidating, it's also a bit alienating. If you aren't a good speaker yourself, you have a great deal of difficulty deciding whether to believe the presenters.

That's why it's important to "de-slick" your show, and there are several ways to do this. My favorite tactic is to put a poor presenter up for five minutes or so, in the number-two or -three spot. I usually try to find an attractive junior executive—eager, knowledgeable on his or her topic, and enthusiastic about participating, but not a polished speaker. It's all right for this junior to be somewhat awkward on his feet—it's even better if he is. Put a junior up to fumble a few lines—just briefly, not for very long—and your prospect's heart will be won over. He'll likely be thinking, "That's what I would be like if I had to do this." It can do wonders for the tension in the room.

The point is that in any team of prospects there is almost certainly going to be *someone* on their side of the table who feels particularly insecure in the presence of a high concentration of polished speakers. It may be a junior on the prospect's side who most identifies with the junior you showcase for a few minutes. Or it might be someone else, a little higher up. Either way, as long as you don't get carried away with bad presenters, you're going to be getting more than you're giving up.

Another tactic is to create an obvious but not crippling problem with your visual materials. If you're using slides, you might want to load one slide backward, for instance. Make it a title slide, or a slide that isn't critical to understanding the argument, of course. Or if you're relying on flip charts, you might find a place to stick two pages together so they both flip at once, by accident.

When I was at Levine, Huntley I often took a dummy videotape with me to credentials presentations we made outside of New York. My agency was doing four to six credentials presentations a week, mostly in our own offices, but often outside as well. Generally the same people at our agency did these presentations, so we were getting a lot of practice. Sometimes I was by myself. Other times the team included our media director and senior marketing strategist. Occasionally we'd have someone from the creative department as well, but we three were doing an immense amount of presenting.

The usual credentials meeting lasted about an hour, and consisted of a few slides showing our agency philosophy and capabilities, along with a couple of case studies, finishing with a six- to ten-minute videotape showing examples of our television advertising. The only real objective for most of these meetings was to familiarize a prospect with the firm, against the chance that sometime in the next few months or years he would be trying to find another advertising agency resource.

I decided whether to use the dummy tape by paying attention to how the meeting was going during the slide show. If I felt we were just too high up on the slick scale, or if I thought the prospect was still at a distance and not involved, when it came time to play our commercials I would reach into my attaché case, pull out the dummy tape, and insert it into the prospect's machine. This tape didn't work. It had static and noise, but no picture.

At this point the prospect almost always worried that his machine was faulty, and that we had come all the way to his office and wouldn't even be able to show our advertising. But after a minute or two of fooling around with the video and wringing my hands, I would say, "Oh, well, let's try the spare tape." Then I'd bring the spare out and sure enough it played flawlessly.

But be careful not to overdo it. I accidentally overdid it once, when before one presentation to an important prospect I decided to put the very first slide in upside down. I was to handle the introductory part of the meeting, and I figured this would give us just a little bit of humanity to go with the professionalism. But just as the machine was turned on, and before the first slide was shown, the projector bulb blew out. After just a couple of minutes we had it replaced, but then when the first slide came up it was upside down!

 Roadmapping

In any meeting with a client, it's often smart to build some suspense, but in a final presentation to a prospective client, the wrong kind of suspense can be fatal.

Advertising agencies frequently present their creative recommendations to existing clients by orchestrating a meeting into a slowly building, suspenseful drama. First the task, then the marketing insight and strategy, next a

peek at the creative objectives and rationale, and finally—
voilà!—the advertising is revealed!

Unfortunately this kind of suspense-building is almost
always counterproductive when it comes to dealing with
prospects rather than clients.

One agency I consulted for described a new business
presentation they thought they should have won, and
asked me what they had done wrong. It was for a bottled water, and the agency had developed a persuasive
strategy and tag line to go with it. This particular bottled
water was not imported, and not from any spectacularly
interesting natural source either. It was good, clean, ordinary water, pure and simple, and it was sold in a grocery
store at a reasonable price, rather than as a designer
product.

The agency's strategy was oriented around the simple
fact that water is, after all, water. It's a fairly unsophisti-
cated product, and only status-oriented social climbers
would insist on one type of "pure" water over another. It
was, if anything, an anti-yuppie strategy, which was a solid
marketing idea for selling bottled water in the Midwest,
where this water was to be marketed.

The tag line the agency came up with, which was to
appear in all the advertising, was "get real." A nice idea,
overall. They really thought they had it won, but the account went elsewhere, and the advertising done by the

Don Peppers

victorious agency, which was now being run, didn't seem all that great.

"What," they asked me, "did we do wrong?"

It turned out that what they did wrong was not "roadmapping" their presentation for the prospect's benefit. They wanted to build suspense and an element of drama into their presentation, so they held their insightful strategy for the last possible moment. In their final presentation meeting, which lasted two hours, they first took the client through twelve other strategies, each of which was briefly examined on its merits, before being discarded as off target, or not believable, or not meaningful enough, or faulty in some other way.

This agency felt they were zeroing in on their own suggested strategy by process of elimination, but what they were really doing was utterly confusing the prospect. You can almost visualize the prospect expectantly examining each strategy as it is unveiled, wondering whether this is going to be the recommended strategy or not. "Yes, yes, it looks as if this is a good strategy. This is it. This must be it. No, no, of course not. It's not right for us. Wait! Now, here's the right strategy. Here we have it! Great idea! No, no, no. Stupid."

What the agency *should* have done to sell this strategy, even by process of elimination, was create a "roadmap" of the presentation's direction, so that the prospect would always know where it was going. I'm not talking about an agenda. Agendas are great, but they aren't roadmaps.

I'm suggesting the agency could simply have tipped its hat a little about its strategic insight at the beginning of the presentation. Perhaps after a very brief outline of the strategic idea there could have been a board placed in front of the meeting room with the word *Reality* on it. This would not have given away the whole strategy, nor would it have revealed the tag line, which was quite powerful. But with this little roadmap handed out first, they could have argued their case in nearly the same fashion, but much more persuasively.

"We're going to keep coming back to this. We've judged every strategy by it. This is where we're going, but first let's take you through some of the alternatives. . . ."

Had the agency done it this way, they would have had their prospect arguing *with* them rather than against them.

An Unexpected Guest

No matter how much planning and strategizing you do, occasionally someone will be invited to the pitch meeting at the last minute. Despite what your prospect may say, rarely are these unanticipated participants inconsequential. If someone is important enough to have been added to the roster at the last minute, that person often holds the key to winning.

At Levine, Huntley we pitched for New York Air's business and won it in an unusual, unannounced pitch. I had retained a number of marketing contacts within New York Air and its parent, Texas Air, as a result of my employment there two or three years previously. So when the marketing regime at the airline changed one spring, I began a dialogue with the new marketing VP, Bruce.

Eventually, Bruce decided he needed new advertising to promote New York Air's initiative in setting up a major hub at Washington's Dulles airport. He had given the people at his current agency a crack at it, but he was very unhappy with their effort, and he was now under a significant time crunch, with the new schedule's announcement only a few weeks away.

By early August, I was able to talk Bruce into accepting a challenge: He agreed to come to the agency for an hour to explain his task and give us some documentation on the details of his schedule, and we promised to produce some advertising ideas for him, in newspaper and radio, within the week. If he liked our ideas he said he would give us the business. He had no time for a formal agency review, and he already had his current agency, Bloom, taking another crack at it—but he didn't have much confidence they'd generate the kind of hard-hitting campaign he said he really needed.

We met with Bruce the first time on a Monday, and on that Thursday afternoon we presented fourteen different newspaper executions and three radio "rough cuts" that were almost good enough to run without being reproduced. It was a truly phenomenal creative performance by Jay and his partner, Tod. In my several years in and around the airline business, I'd never seen airline advertising with such impact.

Bruce had the same impression. He took about two minutes to catch his breath and then asked us if we could have any of the newspaper ads shot, produced, and inserted in *The New York Times* by the end of the following week. If we could, he said he planned to call Bloom and inform them of his decision on the day prior to the first ad's appearance. We had won the business!

Or so we thought. The following Monday, even as the entire agency was mobilized to meet print and radio production deadlines, Bruce called again. He told me that while we had the business "for sure," there was one executive at the firm—a more senior executive—who had asked him to set up a meeting so that we could take him through our presentation. "Who is this executive?" I asked. It was Frank Lorenzo, CEO of Texas Air. Bruce would like to bring him in the next day.

𝒟ℴ𝓃 𝒫ℯ𝓅𝓅ℯ𝓇𝓈

Naturally our spirits sank. Maybe we celebrated too soon?

We organized the presentation again, and I tried to fill everyone in on what I knew of Frank Lorenzo, since I had worked at Texas Air (for both Texas International and New York Air) for four years. Clearly, I said, Frank was going to be the decision-maker on this. We should not take the business for granted by any means.

We knew we had to make a real presentation. Frank came in with Bruce, and Bruce's boss, the CEO at NYA, a guy named Bob Gallaway. They all came in, plus Frank had somebody else with him. This was a man I had never met before, although I had heard of him. He was Doug Birdsall, the senior vice president of marketing at Continental Airlines, one of Frank's recently acquired airlines.

Frank introduced Doug by saying, "Well, you know I just happened to be in town with Doug, and I thought he might like to come by and see your presentation. So if you don't mind, he'll just sit in our meeting, no big deal."

Right away I took aside the other team members who were presenting, Bob Schmidt and Jim Dragoumis, and said, "You know this isn't like Frank to have an informal, unplanned arrival by anybody. My suggestion is we be very careful with Doug Birdsall and we might even go so far as pitching the presentation to him. It wouldn't surprise me if Frank isn't going to rely on Doug's judgment on this, because I think Bruce is an unseasoned marketing guy, but Doug has a reputation as a marketing expert."

So we focused our energies on Doug, which flattered the heck out of him. At the end of the meeting, Frank, Bob, Doug, and Bruce went out for a little while, and then came back in. Frank said, "Okay, you have the business."

Two weeks later, Bruce and I were at the U.S. Open (attending premier sporting events with clients is one of the privileges of being in the advertising business), and Bruce got an emergency phone call from his office.

After he took the call, he came back and said, "Well, we have a new president at New York Air. His name is Doug Birdsall."

Chapter 14
▼▼▼▼▼▼▼

Rehearsing

Rehearsing. You've gotta do it. Just don't overdo it.

If your staff is inexperienced in public speaking, it is generally true that the more you rehearse, the better. But, like training for a marathon, too many rehearsals can be exhausting. If your presentation runs a couple of hours and you rehearse all the way through more than once or twice, you'll not only wear yourself out, you'll peak too soon.

But there is one area in which rehearsals are guaranteed to improve your performance. The most difficult parts of any coordinated presentation are not the individual speakers' parts, but the transitions from one speaker to another. If you concentrate on polishing the transitions, you will get ninety percent of the roughness out.

Here's what you do:

First run through a full rehearsal. Everyone should give his or her planned speech, which should always be extemporaneous. Never let anybody read anything.

Then rehearse only the transitions. If your presentation includes Jack, Jerry, and Sally, for instance, start with Jack's first-minute opening up and then his last minute, which presumably includes a lead into Jerry's topic. Then comes Jerry's first minute and last minute, and finally Sally's first and last.

You can rehearse a two-hour presentation like that in ten or fifteen minutes, and you can do it several times without wearing out your team.

Transitions reveal how cohesive your staff is and whether they are team players or simply a collection of individuals. If the presentation team is a multioffice group, people who literally just met each other yesterday, rehearsing transitions is critical.

How to Make Better Extemporaneous Presentations

■ *Bring a home video camera and tripod in to tape the presentation rehearsal. Let everyone see how they look and sound. Nearly everyone will be astounded, so be sure to do this early on.*

■ *During the presentation, always look people in the eye. Pretend you're having a conversation with one or more members of your audience, then look at them and talk to them! Don't look down—never look people in their chests, or their mouths. Look only in their eyes, and don't look away.*

■ *Stand up and give your talk, and walk around if it won't look bad, but don't pace back and forth. If you have extra nervous energy, practice clenching and unclenching the toes of each foot, right-left, right-left.*

■ *If you think you'll be nervous when your turn comes to speak, then prior to the presentation you should spend some time memorizing, perfectly, the first sixty seconds or so of your talk. To do this you should first speak it (perhaps to a tape machine),* and then write it down word for word. After that, just go over it, and over it, and over it, until you absolutely, positively, won't forget it. Word for word.

- If you need notes (after the first minute or two), use big writing on small cards, so you'll never have to search for your place. Practice going through your note cards. Make sure every new thought has its own card.

- Relax. If you are nervous prior to speaking, take a series of deep breaths, then practice in your head the first ten to fifteen words you will say. Go over, in your mind, how to say them. Concentrate only on hearing your own words, with the emphasis you plan to use.

- Smile. Presenting is hard work, but you have to make it look easy.

Mistakes Often Made in Pitch Presentations

- Repeating what someone else has already said.
- Overlooking the specific assignment.
- Not having a clear fix on the amount of time

you are likely to need at every point. (Hint: Have markers in your presentation, based on the rehearsal, so you know when John gets up there should be seventy-five minutes left, and so forth.)

- *Self-worship.*
- *Failing to rehearse how to answer questions.*
- *Disagreeing with one another.*

Chapter 15

▼▼▼▼▼▼▼

The No-Notes Presentation

At every company I've ever worked with or consulted for, both in and out of the advertising business, presentations are done with visual aids. Slides, overheads, flip charts—the purpose of these aids is to help the audience follow the line of argument.

However, in most such meetings, the visual aids really turn out to be more for the benefit of the presenters. The bullet points on the slides remind the presenter of what points to emphasize in the case study, and the order of the overheads disciplines the direction of the discussion.

The single most persuasive way to pitch is not to *present* but to *discuss* your issues with a prospect. Think of the event not as a presentation, but as a meeting. And meetings are a lot more interesting, more involving, than presentations are.

But in a pitch meeting you have a message to get across. You need to address whatever issues the prospect asked you to address, and you have to *persuade* the prospect. So even if you want to adopt a meeting format, you'll still have to do a lot of the talking—probably most of the talking—in a pitch presentation.

There are ways to dramatize your pitch, however, and increase its persuasiveness, by minimizing the use of visual aids. My all-time favorite highly persuasive pitch format is what I call the "no-notes" presentation. This is a format I first saw at Lintas's subsidiary in Canada, a super shop with an extremely good new-business track record.

Imagine this: Ten executives—five from the prospect organization and five from your firm—go into your conference room to sit down around a table. As they enter, your own executives pick up place names to identify themselves. But the conference table has ten identical place settings, each with a clean pad and pen for taking notes, a glass of water, and an agenda for the meeting.

The seating arrangement is quite casual, so the prospect executives pick their own chairs according to their own personal preferences. If you have to show video, you may point out the best seats for being able to see it. Your own people mix in among the prospect executives. No one

from your firm carries anything at all. The prospect executives will likely bring out notebooks, or binders with the
selection team's checklist, or something like that.

But your own executives have absolutely no notes, no
handouts, no overheads, flip charts or decks—nothing.
When they sit down, all they have in front of them is the
clean pad of paper, agenda, pen, and glass of water that's
already at every place.

You open the meeting by calling everyone's attention to
the agenda, which outlines the issues the prospect has
assigned you to cover, your objectives for the meeting,
and some suggested time breaks for getting from one
topic to the next. But you emphasize that this meeting will
remain flexible, so you can accommodate questions and
contributions from the prospect company at any time.
You're looking your prospects in the eye. You watch for
reactions, feedback.

After everyone on your team is introduced, putting the
name placard on the table in front of his or her seat, you
spend ten minutes on an overview of your firm, if any is
needed, and then you turn to one of your associates and
ask her to tell the company about the work done for such-
and-such client. The associate talks animatedly about this
work, using figures and facts, but she never looks down at
her notes at all, because she has none. No one does. She
simply looks the prospect executives in the eye the way

you did, and she covers the case study. It's not memorized, it's conversational. It may take her five minutes, or it might take twenty.

You interrupt her at one point and ask her to go into more detail about one item or another. She gets up and goes to the far wall, picks up a copy of the ad being discussed, in order to show the prospects still sitting at the table. She may also have a bar chart of results, just to illustrate the dramatic increases she was talking about. She says this particular case is interesting because the distribution problems are similar to those the prospect faces. When she says this she turns to a couple of the prospects and asks if they agree or not.

The meeting goes for two hours, and none of you ever resorts to so much as a three-by-five card, yet the case studies and data you cover are quite detailed.

The no-notes presentation format, in my opinion, is absolutely one of the most persuasive kinds of pitch meetings you can have, *particularly* because you're up against two or five competitors who will almost certainly use decks, slides, and other visual aids to steer their discussion.

But how do you choreograph this kind of meeting? Two hours of presenting and no one gets to use notes? How do you prepare for it?

It's very simple, actually. Create your presentation *with*

visual aids first. Everyone should have a deck, either written by themselves or written for them, however you normally do it. Each deck of pages should have the same bullet points the presenter would make if he were leading the discussion with overheads or slides. No need to create the overheads, however. For the rehearsal, just speak from the written deck. Sit around the table and go through the presentation once, for timing. Rehearse the transitions three or four times to make sure it flows from presenter to presenter.

Then tell everyone to go away for an hour, take out fifty percent of the pages from their own deck, and return for another rehearsal. They'll have to make the same points they just made—the ones on the current, complete deck —and in the same basic order, but with half the pages. No additional writing is allowed on the remaining pages.

When they go through it again, and get it right, tell them to go away for another hour and return with only one page of notes, which they can write up however they like. After this run-through, the next (and last) rehearsal will be without even that single page.

In these rehearsals I tell people to imagine they just met the prospect at a cocktail party, and now they're simply explaining their case study to him.

The only time a visual aid is allowed in a no-notes meeting is when it is absolutely essential to make a point

Don Peppers

clear—a chart or graph, perhaps, or a map, or a picture, but absolutely no word charts with bullet points.

The no-notes presentation format isn't appropriate for every situation, and often it won't be practical, but when you can manage it, it's a highly persuasive device. It's my very favorite type of pitch meeting.

Chapter 16

▼▼▼▼▼▼

Some Tips for Managing Pitch Meetings

aking a pitch meeting work is not the same as making any other meeting work. Pitches need to be planned, rehearsed, reorganized, drilled, and planned again. You have to cover all the prospect's requirements, understand and focus on the key issues, and deal with the individual and group psychology at work in the room. You have to be able to handle questions, and you have to look like a team when you're doing it, not a collection of individuals.

These things require planning, preparation, and management. Someone has to *make* it happen, the right way and on time. To make sure your pitch goes according to plan, follow these guidelines:

1. **Appoint a pitch "ayatollah."** We frequently hear leaders referred to as "czars"—like the "education czar" or the "drug czar." But for my money, the word *czar* does not connote enough religious and moral authority for the kinds of tasks that anyone who runs a pitch meeting must accomplish. So, when you begin preparing for a pitch, appoint an ayatollah who will be the absolute, no-appeal, sole arbiter of disputes and conflict in developing the presentation.

Your goal is to look like a team, not a collection of individuals. The ayatollah's job is to make decisions about what gets presented, what doesn't, and how the meeting should flow. The goal is for your presentation to look as if everything came out of one mind, even though it may involve five or six presenters, and probably came out of ten different minds at your firm.

The chairman or CEO of your firm should take everyone aside early on in the process and say something like "Folks, for the purpose of this pitch to the XYZ Corporation, I've asked Molly to be our ayatollah. She has my proxy, and I won't reverse her no matter whose feelings are hurt. But please don't hold it against her. She doesn't mean to be dictatorial, but if we're going to get this done well and on time, someone has to be the boss. For the next three months on this project, it's her. Period."

2. Get the client involved. Getting the prospect to interact and participate in the meeting will do wonders for putting him at ease, improving chemistry, and persuading him. Here are some ideas:

■ *Open the meeting to general conversation, recapping objectives and expectations. Get the prospect to answer simple yes/no questions at first, like "Is this correct?" or "You agree?" But within minutes you should be able to ask him to elaborate with a "why" or "how" or "what else" question.*

■ *Modularize your presentation and offer to start with whatever section the prospect most wants to hear first. When he states his preference, ask him to explain briefly why he prefers to start there.*

■ *Embed your presentation with questions, and ask the prospect to guess the answers. What kind of response do you think this ad drew? How many lawyers do you think the other side employed?*

■ *Interact vigorously with your presentation materials. Circle things on your flip charts, draw freehand diagrams. If the prospect makes a point about one of your pictures, give him the marker and see if he wants to make his point more clearly.*

3. Don't prolong a conversation once your objective is achieved. When a prospect agrees with you on something, let it stand. Don't try to get more. At Lintas I once had a prospect in our conference room, and one of our creative directors was showing him potential print-ad executions for his product. As she showed him the second print ad, he paused and said, "That is without a doubt the most insightful headline about our product I've ever seen. It's terrific! Did you do that?" She responded, "Yes, I did, and thank you! But now let me show you what else we've done too. . . ."

4. Have a clear plan for handling the unexpected. As tightly structured as the meeting is, and as comfortable as you are with your own material, a smart prospect will try to throw a curve at some point, just to test your ability to think on your feet. Before the meeting, rehearse how to answer questions, who will answer them on what topics, and who will direct the discussion when it goes in an unplanned direction.

5. Don't let an account executive present a case study on his own client. The account executive who works on a piece of business will know too much about it. She'll go into way too much detail, and she's quite liable to reveal mistakes made on the account simply to discuss the solutions that resulted. You know how the best math teacher in high school is someone who had trouble with the subject herself? The same is true for case studies. If you plan to talk about your success with one of your accounts, get an executive who is not already familiar with it. In order to present it, she'll have to learn it from scratch, and she'll be much better prepared to explain it.

Chapter 17

▼▼▼▼▼▼

Zen and the Art of Pitch Management

E ver read *Zen and the Art of Motorcycle Maintenance?* It's a terrific book, and I urge you to read it in order to prepare yourself for the long string of disappointments you'll almost certainly face once you get seriously into the business of managing pitches.

Zen and the Art of Motorcycle Maintenance centers around the author's philosophical search for a definition of "quality." His basic premise is that if the only reason you ever get under your motorcycle and tinker with it is to fix something that's wrong, so it will run better, then your motorcycle will always be breaking down. But if you genuinely *enjoy* the process of tinkering with your motorcycle, so you're always fooling around with it whether it needs fixing or not, then your motorcycle will run more smoothly and dependably.

That's my philosophy of pitch management. If the only reason you get into it is to win pitches—if that's your sole criterion of success and enjoyment—then you're very unlikely to win many competitions. However, if you *enjoy* the process of pitching, and if you gain some benefit from the *process* of pitching, then pretty soon you'll be winning a greater and greater proportion of your contests.

So concentrate first, not on simply winning this particular competition, but on managing the pitch meeting *process* itself. You can't expect to win every pitch, so you might as well not plan on it. But you *can* get value out of every pitch, provided that you treat each one as an opportunity to rachet the learning curve a little further up. My simple equation for whether or not a pitch was successful is this: After the pitch, you should honestly be able to say, "Wow! That was the best we've ever done."

In my consulting business, when I'm asked to help a firm manage a pitch, this is the barometer of success I use. Frequently a client will want to pay me something less up front, and give me more if they get the business. But getting the business is still going to be a matter of luck, to a large extent. The variables are just too complicated. So if I agree to work on a contingency basis at all, I tell my client they must decide whether to give me the

Don Peppers

bonus payment immediately after the pitch meeting concludes, but *before* the prospect has made a decision. If my client can honestly say that this pitch meeting was the best they have ever done, then I should get the bonus.

If you can enjoy the process, and concentrate simply on making every pitch meeting better than the last one, your batting average will gradually, but definitely, improve.

Ironically, this means tolerating mistakes. Whoever your "pitch ayatollah" is, he or she will probably know a lot more about the psychology, choreography, and, perhaps, even the substance of the pitch than many others on the team. But the members of your pitch team are likely to be a pretty strong-willed bunch of senior executives. So situations will arise in which the pitch ayatollah knows that doing a case study one way will be more persuasive than another way, or making the strategic explanation come second this time, instead of first, will be better. And sometimes, even though the pitch manager knows better, the right thing to do might be just to let an insistent team member make a mistake, in order to generate learning.

Obviously, whenever possible you want to demonstrate to the team member what's wrong with this approach during the rehearsal for the pitch. However, it isn't always possible to do so. Some things simply require the dynamic of a live presentation with a real prospect in the room. If this is the case, rather than dictate a change to a resisting team member, a smart pitch manager will allow the team member to do it his way for this pitch. Then, following the pitch—and *before* the decision is given by the prospect—the pitch ayatollah should take the team member aside and show just how the presentation would have been improved had it been done her way instead.

Pitch management is a skill. If you want to improve it over time, if you want to continue to rachet up the learning curve, you have to tolerate mistakes in order to learn from them. Any mistake that won't generate a learning experience is just a mistake. It has no redeeming value.

Chapter 18

▼▼▼▼▼▼

Off to See the Wizard

There is a famous scene in *The Wizard of Oz* in which Dorothy, having been admitted into the Emerald City, is reverently and somewhat fearfully conversing with the wizard—or a representation of him in the form of a man's face projected onto a huge movie screen immediately in front of her, his voice thundering out at her from a set of loudspeakers.

While she's desperately trying to deal with this giant being, Dorothy's little dog Toto wanders off to the side wall a few feet away and draws a small curtain aside, revealing the back of a little man manipulating this image of himself at a control panel. He turns briefly, discovers what the dog has done, pulls the curtain closed again, and then the wizard's face is shown roaring, "Pay no attention to the man behind the curtain . . ."

This is the scene that comes to my mind whenever I think about the lengths to which ad agency pitch teams will go just to explain the "rational" process they went through in developing the advertising they're showing.

Clients have different needs. Some want big-budget, safely warm and musical advertising, some want humorous or cute advertising, and some want holy-shit-I-can't-believe-they-really-did-that advertising. But *every* client wants *creativity* from his agency. And the creative process —which is really what the client is paying for—is something that will almost certainly remain a mystery to him.

This is because it's impossible to capture the essence of the creative process with any kind of rational description. Creativity is magic, plain and simple. If the process were *rationally* understandable, it wouldn't really be "creative" —right?

The real way to get creative advertising is to hire creative people. You want more creativity? Hire people who are even more creative. It's that simple. And how do you know if the people you hire are going to be creative? Because the advertising they do will be creative, that's how. It's just like Will Rogers's advice on making money in the stock market. First you buy a stock, then when it goes up you sell it. If it doesn't go up, don't buy it.

But think about the dilemma this poses for a potential client trying to evaluate an advertising agency. You can show the prospect all sorts of advertising work already created for your other clients. You can talk persuasively and at great length about your staff's creative capabilities. Sooner or later, however, the prospect is likely to say to himself, "Sure, I know they did some great commercials for the XYZ corporation, and the other advertising they've shown me looks terrific. But how do I really know they'll be able to do the same kind of creative work for me?"

In the back of his mind the prospect's wrestling with his own advertising problems which, to him, seem totally intractable. If it were any other way—if he already knew what his commercial should look like to achieve his marketing objectives—then he wouldn't be sitting there in your conference room trying to decide whether to give you his business, would he? He'd be busy producing the advertising he knows would work.

So not only is your prospect already nervous, intimidated, and maybe a little scared to be sitting where he is, he has no idea how to think about what it is you really do. His career might hang in the balance, as well as the fortunes of his brand or his company. He might be eager to give you his account, in the hope that you'll solve his problem and make him a hero at the same time.

But he doesn't yet understand, rationally, just *how* the

advertising he likes—the advertising you showed him—was actually thought up. And until he can visualize this, until he has at least some understanding of how you're going to go about inventing a solution for him that's every bit as creative and innovative, and how you're going to do it again the next time, and the next, he's going to continue to be nervous and edgy.

In many professional-services situations, the dilemma is similar. If your business requires selling something that's difficult to explain or involves a great deal of technical expertise, whether it's developing legal defenses, generating corporate strategy, or putting together PC networks, your prospect will have the same basic concern. You can tout your legal work for other clients, you can show referrals from them, or you can talk about the cases you've won —but in the final analysis your prospect will be wondering if you can do the same thing for him. And there's no way to explain this dilemma away.

Blue Beads

This is where I fall back on an advertising principle called "permission to believe." You need to give your client some sort of rational *permission* to believe you know what you're doing, and therefore you can do it again for him.

To give him this permission, you have to explain *something* to him. You can't just say, "Yeah, creativity's really magic, isn't it?"

Instead, you say something like "Okay, here's our process for developing advertising: First, we do Step A. Then we follow up with Step B. With the right kind of feedback —see this diagram?—we go right to Step C, but sometimes we repeat Step B." And so forth, and so on.

All agencies, big and small alike, tell their prospects— and their clients—they use some kind of structured, rational, creative development "process" to generate executions that really are creative. Step A. Step B. For the most part, however, these processes are just so much filler. They bear only a token resemblance to the actual process, which the agency executives themselves don't really understand anyway.

Chiat/Day, for instance, uses a process called account planning. Now, Chiat is one of the most creative advertising agencies in the business. But one thing this means is that the dilemma a prospect faces when he's thinking about hiring Chiat/Day is particularly acute.

The account-planning process is an idea Chiat imported from British advertising agencies. It relies on extensive, qualitative consumer research (i.e., focus groups) conducted prior to the creatives starting their work. This research is the thing that's supposed to yield the unique insights enabling Chiat's creatives to develop their advertising concepts.

But the truth is, while account planning can certainly help keep a creative execution "on strategy"—any research will do that—it has absolutely nothing at all to do with the *creative* process itself. Chiat's creativity occurs because the agency hires highly creative people, and maintains a work environment that allows their creativity to flourish. Or maybe it's something else, who knows?

Similar stories could be told at every other agency I know of. Each one uses some sort of rational process to explain to mystified prospects just how they go about generating advertising that is genuinely creative. The more creative the agency is, in general, the more useful such a process is—for explaining it, not for doing it. Because the truth is, like the bumper sticker, creativity happens. You *can't* explain it. And sometimes it doesn't happen.

Nevertheless, if a highly creative advertising execution is thought up, an agency's pitch team will *reverse-engineer* everything in the pitch meeting—strategy, research findings, creative-development process, and the like—to justify the execution. In fact, I've never worked at any agency where we *didn't* reverse-engineer the strategy and process —frequently. See? We arrived at this brilliantly creative ad by following our unique, proprietary method—Step A, Step B, Step C.

I don't really think this represents any kind of ethical lapse. It's just trying to give prospects permission to believe that the brilliant, original, creative idea we just showed them was actually produced in a creativity factory. Now, even though you can't build this creativity factory yourself, you see, we can at least show you how our factory works.

The research director at Lintas, Jan Homan, called this the "blue beads" principle. A couple of decades ago a detergent manufacturer came up with a new, improved version of its detergent. The detergent really was new and improved, but it looked like exactly the same stuff as before. So the company put little blue beads—placebos— into the detergent to make it *look* different. The blue beads did nothing for the effectiveness of the detergent, but they gave consumers *permission* to believe the soap was new and improved.

Personally, I've always been reminded of the little man manipulating the wizard's image for Dorothy's benefit.

Chapter 19

▼▼▼▼▼▼▼

A Word About Integrity

'll never forget the first time I encountered the Big Lie in a selling situation. I was at Compton Advertising, an agency whose name has since been submerged entirely under the weight of too many mergers and acquisitions. It was my very first involvement with a pitch for a new client.

The pitch team, which was to include me, was gathered in the agency's main conference room to rehearse for the next day's presentation. My role was to present a case study of British Airways' highly acclaimed global advertising campaign, shot by the Saatchis (Compton's new British parent). It was one of the first times a single set of television commercials had actually been run in a large number of countries around the world, with only the language of the voice-over changed. At Compton, I managed BA's campaign in the United States.

This was my first experience in the advertising agency industry, and I'd been enjoying myself immensely. There was a good deal of speaking and presenting involved in the advertising business, mostly to clients, and I liked to perform. I had fewer doubts about my own abilities in this new situation than Phil did.

Phil was the pitch leader, a more senior Compton executive who was now drilling the various presenters and quizzing them as to how they might handle different situations. Not only was Phil a very senior executive and a skillful "new business" hand at Compton, he had an infamous reputation as a management bully with an explosive temper. We were all gun-shy in his presence.

The pitch we were making was a simple, straightforward presentation of two or three case studies, including mine. I remember vividly how one of my peers was rehearsing his presentation. Phil very much wanted this particular case to demonstrate something specifically aimed at the retail nature of the prospective client's business, and my friend Tom was having difficulty making the point.

Finally, Phil lost his patience. He told Tom to finish the case study with a proclamation that the advertising had generated an immediate surge of more than eight percent in retail demand for the product. This would show that the agency could put together a campaign that had both long-term brand benefits and short-term sales effects. He told Tom to talk to the art department about generating the appropriate bar chart to illustrate the point.

There was a pause. Tom finally said something to the effect that retail sales hadn't increased eight percent. In fact, there hadn't been any increase in retail sales. It was customer awareness that had increased eight percent and that was in a research study that had been conducted two quarters later.

Phil looked at Tom like he had just landed on Venus. Then he said, "I don't give a f--- what really happened! *Lie* about it, okay? *Is that okay???*"

And Tom did lie about it. Apparently Tom was used to this. This was war, here. We wanted to win a new client. We deserved this new client. We would do what we had to do.

I remember this incident as if it happened just yesterday. It was the first time I realized how sleazy the selling business could be, if you just let it happen.

What struck me most about the whole thing was the utter casualness with which a detailed lie was fabricated and told to a set of company executives whose trust we were trying to earn.

This particular time I had no way not to let it happen. I certainly wasn't going to bet my new career on a showdown with the venomous Phil. Not only infamous for his temper, he was also well known for settling scores. And although he wasn't my direct boss, he was very clearly senior to me.

More than a decade later, as a successful consultant with my own company and a track record filled with pitches won and lost, I still reflect on this incident often, and on the whole issue of the Big Lie. I don't tolerate it in any pitch I give.

But in the advertising business we all knew that lying was not an uncommon occurrence. One story was real and one was created for the client's benefit. One reality was accurate and correct, but for internal consumption only, while a different reality was employed to deal with the client.

In my view, it's one thing to emphasize some aspect of your sales message you know to have a special appeal to your client or prospective client, but it's another thing entirely to make up a bald-faced, highly specific lie designed solely to win a prospect's confidence, or to take his business simply by deceiving him.

Three Simple Principles

In my very first job after leaving the air force, when I went to work for American Independent Oil Company as an economist, my boss gave me three simple principles to follow in making career decisions. He said these were Jack Sunderland's "rules of business." Jack was the president of the company. If I just paid attention to these three principles, my boss told me, everything else would follow. His principles were:

- *Make money.*
- *Have fun.*
- *Be ethical.*

That simple.

But the more you compete with others for business, the more difficult it will become to decide exactly what's ethical and what's not. Our society was built squarely on the idea that the greater social good is achieved by allowing competition to flourish. Competition drives our economic system, it drives our legal system, and it drives our political system. Competition drives our society, and that means we are all pitching, all the time.

We are all *advocates* who live and work within the framework of this culture. So ask yourself: Would it be ethical for a lawyer to refuse to represent or defend someone he knows to be guilty? Is a legislator behaving unethically when he trades his vote with his opponent on an issue he considers not so critical, in order to get a better chance at passing a law he considers more important? Or what of the investment banker or loan officer pushing to complete a less-than-perfect deal in order to secure a commission for his firm before his competitors succeed? Is it unethical for an advertising executive to do his best possible job promoting a product when he knows the product isn't as good as one of its competitors?

Or consider the often-raised issue of "the appearance of propriety." *Appearing* ethical has nothing to do with *being* ethical. Appearing ethical is certainly good business practice, but *being* ethical is a very personal decision and involves self-knowledge, not projections or appearances.

So deciding what is or isn't ethical isn't so simple after all. It's easy to determine whether you're having fun at your job, and it's usually not too difficult to identify the business strategy likely to make more money, but deciding whether the action you plan to take is ethical or not is often a much more complex issue.

Still, I think business competition can be fought according to certain rules of fair play that allow you to compete vigorously while still having no trouble getting to sleep at night. Maybe what I'm really talking about is what some philosophers call "situational ethics"—the idea that the ethics behind an action are determined in large part by the situation (or even the industry) in which the action takes place.

Think about it. Some actions are totally, unquestionably, wrong or unethical. If, for instance, you were to encounter a competitor and viciously knock him to the ground in order to gain an advantage, everyone would consider this absolutely unethical, right? Of course they would. Unless your business was professional football. Pro football is a situation in which knocking a competitor to the ground, even viciously, is not considered unethical. Knocking a ref to the ground, or knocking your own teammate to the ground to hog a winning play—*that* would be unethical.

But what about lying and deception? Surely everyone would agree this is universally wrong, isn't it?

The simple answer is no. Lying and deception are as acceptable in *some* business situations as knocking someone to the ground is in football situations. Every business, for instance, wants to deceive its competitors. There really do have to be secrets in business, as there are in almost any form of competition. No one would criticize Procter & Gamble for deceiving Unilever about its intention to introduce a new product. And no one would argue that United should be totally honest with Delta in discussing its plan to cut or raise the price on flights to Florida.

The fact is, there's not a lot of difference between being honest with your competitors and being guilty of criminal collusion. In any large business, antitrust rules actually *require* you to be less than candid with competitors.

But what about clients? Surely it's always unethical to lie to your own customer or client, whose interests you are supposed to be respecting?

The answer again is no. I think it's unethical in most business situations, but there are even some legitimate commercial transactions that depend on deceiving a customer, provided you are acting in the customer's interest. When a doctor prescribes a placebo for his client, what is he doing? He's lying. And no one would seriously accuse him of being unethical, because his deception is in the interest of his patient.

So how do you sort out these issues? How do you determine, in a sudden-death fight for some customer's business, what's ethical and what's not?

As a rainmaker, I've found myself faced with literally scores of ethical dilemmas. To deceive or not to deceive? To buy information or not? To pay finder's fees or not?

So I developed four basic ethical principles for helping me determine whether a particular action is ethical or not.

I think these principles apply to almost any "situation" involving business competition.

1. Full disclosure is the best policy.

Anything that can be done openly and publicly without embarrassment is inherently ethical. I know of no exception to this rule. But the converse is *not* true—things that must remain secret aren't necessarily unethical. Competition inherently involves secrecy, and even deception.

2. Aiding or abetting someone else who is acting unethically is itself unethical.

I am sometimes approached by someone who promises to recommend my firm provided we agree to pay a finder's fee if we get the business. Paying a commission or finder's fee to secure business is not unethical on its face. But if I have reason to suspect the recipient is deceiving his principal, I am just as guilty as he is. (One way to sort this dilemma out is to use the "disclosure" principle. If someone asks for a finder's fee, ask for a letter from his client authorizing him to collect such a fee.)

3. Respect your fiduciary responsibilities, to your employer, your employees, your stockholders, and your clients.

It is unethical to betray the trust of those whose interests we are being paid to represent. This can be a complex issue in any personal-services business. Fiduciary responsibilities are the second edge of the two-edged ethical sword. For instance, if I choose not to pursue a casino business or a tobacco account because it would violate my own personal ethical standards, I first need to balance that decision against the economic interests of my employer or stockholders. Discussing these issues with my employer in advance of having to make decisions about them would help immensely.

4. Don't tolerate a competitive playing field that isn't level.

I think anyone who believes in and profits from the free-market system is honor bound not to undermine it. This rule covers a wide territory. No collusion with your competitors, for instance. And don't deny economic opportunities to others for reasons such as race, gender, or religion. Most companies are committed at least philosophically to the belief that a free-market system is beneficial to us all. So it would be an act of sheer hypocrisy to deny someone access to this system for reasons of sex or color.

What Would You Do?

When I was at Levine, Huntley, Patti Goldrick and I wrote an ethics questionnaire which was printed

in *Advertising Age* and became a hot topic in the
ad community for several weeks. People were com-
paring notes, arguing about the right answers, and
so forth.

The questions below, rewritten to encompass
more business situations than mere advertising, are
similar to the ones that appeared in *Ad Age*. What
would you do in each of these situations? Once
you've gone through all the questions and you're
sure you can figure out each, see *Solutions to Ethics Questionnaire* on page 255.

1. You're competing with two other firms for an
accounting relationship with the Magnasonic Consumer Electronics company. Its chief rival is Rolavision, and Rolavision's director of accounting
worked in the same position at Magnasonic for several years before joining Rolavision a few months
ago. He is still on extremely good terms with
Magnasonic's CFO. You hire him as a partner, specifically to work on the Magnasonic pitch, with a
promise that he'll be kept on even if the pitch fails,
and paid a bonus if it succeeds.

Ethical or unethical?

2. You and three other vendors are competing
for a multimillion-dollar telecommunications ser-

vices contract with a large midwestern firm with offices around the world. The pitch involves not just price, but also management help, consulting, and other value-added services in connection with this firm's overall communications program. Late one evening, a couple of days before the scheduled presentation, you are proofing your slides at a slide supply house. By accident you are handed a fairly complete set of slides put together by your chief rival, for the same pitch.

You have enough time to examine their slides, get the gist of it, and understand your competitor's pricing strategy before the slide house manager realizes his mistake and retrieves the file. He's very embarrassed about the mistake. You return to your office, change your presentation so as to attack your competitor directly, and undercut his pricing without revealing to anyone that you have this new information.

Ethical or unethical?

3. Same as Question 2, but your competitor's slides weren't handed to you. You see the file folder on a work table near you. After waiting for the supplier to leave the room you peek at them.

Ethical or unethical?

4. Your small direct-mail firm is looking to hire

a senior account management person. You interview a manager at a competitive firm who promises to bring with him one of your rival's biggest accounts if you hire him at the salary he's asking. His salary demand is quite large compared to the level of the job, but it would clearly be a good investment in terms of winning this particular account. You hire him, and the account comes to you.

Ethical or unethical?

5. Your financial services organization has been invited to compete for the right to handle a very large retail chain's pension fund. The chain's autocratic founder is seventy-five years old and, in past discussions, you've come away with the impression that he is very narrow-minded too. Every senior manager on this CEO's staff is white, male, and at least fifty-five years old.

A few weeks ago your firm lost a big piece of pension-fund business that was overseen by one of your brightest talents. So far you haven't been able to redeploy this manager, but this particular account would be perfect. Only one problem: Your manager is a thirty-year-old Oriental female, and you're absolutely positive both your competitors will be putting up older white males. Your best guess is if you put this account manager on the job, you can't win the business. So you don't.

Ethical or unethical?

6. You're in the executive recruitment business, and a good friend of yours calls to say a colleague of his is looking for a firm to put on retainer for a large assignment. This colleague is apparently reviewing a number of headhunters, but your friend says he's sure he can deliver the account to you, in exchange for a finder's fee of fifteen percent of your first year's fee income on the business. If the contract is as large as he says it is, your fee income may approach $200,000. You agree to pay him if you get the business.

Ethical or unethical?

7. You're an account executive at a graphic arts firm, headed to a presentation to a client. Your boss (the vice president) and the creative director at your firm are in a heated discussion about whether to show two different design schemes for this assignment or just one. You think this client's interests would be better served if you showed both the ideas you were bringing with you, but they finally decide to show just one, in order to demonstrate the firm's genuine commitment to it. They plan to

keep the other one in the portfolio bag. At the
meeting the client seems to like the one he's
shown, but then he turns to you and asks you point-
blank if you brought any other ideas. What do you
tell him?

Three

▾▾▾▾▾▾

Pros-
pecting

Chapter 20

▼▼▼▼▼▼▼

The Two Stages of Prospecting

Pitching is fun, some would even say glamorous.

But the truth is, the most successful pitches are usually waged by those who have already laid the most careful, methodical groundwork. The advantage goes to those who have access to the most information and intelligence resources, who have the strongest network of contacts nurtured over the years, and the largest assortment of *relationships* with prospective clients.

To lay the right groundwork, you mostly have to rely on a thorough, well-executed prospecting program, and that's what the rest of this book is about. We'll be talking about making contact with people at firms you'd like to do business with, and then keeping them on speaking terms with your company for the months or years it might take before their company's account goes into play—if it ever does.

Prospecting should be thought of, really, as two different kinds of activities:

1. Outreach, and
2. Prospect management.

Outreach is the stage that most people will recognize as prospecting. In this stage of prospecting your goal is to reach people you've never met, who have responsibility over the budgets and purchase decisions that will affect your business.

But prospect management—managing your relationships once you've made contact—is also critical.

Unfortunately, the skills needed for outreach and prospect management are entirely different from those necessary for pitching itself. If pitching is hunting, then prospecting is farming.

And even though an accomplished hunter may become a hero, a good farmer almost always eats better.

Chapter 21

▼▼▼▼▼▼▼

Prospecting Outreach: The Proton Theory

One of my hobbies is reading about cosmology, the search for the origins of the universe. Cosmologists are now searching for a new theory linking all the known forces—gravity, electromagnetism, and nuclear forces. But like quantum theory and relativity, any new theory will be accepted only if it can be shown to predict something quantitatively measurable.

According to Stephen Hawking's book *A Brief History of Time,* one prediction of most "grand unified theories" is that the proton is not a totally stable particle, after all. Until now, it was always assumed the proton would *never* "fly apart at the seams" without some cause. But the new theories, if correct, predict that even a proton has a chance of coming apart on its very own—but it's a very small chance. In any given year the chance a particular proton will spontaneously self-destruct is about one in a million trillion trillion. So even if you were to follow a particular proton around from the beginning to the end of the universe, you would still have only an infinitesimal chance of seeing it decay.

But: If you put a million trillion trillion protons in a deep, dark vat several miles under Utah, and set up detectors to spot any flashes indicating spontaneous proton decays, chances are you'll see one every year or so—*if* these new theories are correct.

That's why I call my theory of prospecting the proton theory. Don't try to build your business by following a single prospect around, waiting for his relationship with his current vendor to split apart. Rather, you should have enough prospects under observation so you'll be on the scene when a few of those relationships come undone.

To collect enough protons for your vat, you have to be an active prospector. But what exactly is "prospecting"? In some businesses, prospecting means looking for immediate sales. In other businesses, prospecting means trying to develop sales *leads*.

But in advertising, and in most other businesses that sell large-budget, infrequently purchased products or services to other businesses, the idea of prospecting is not to generate immediate sales, or even to find sales leads, per se. Instead, the first thing a prospector tries to do is develop personal contacts at companies that eventually might be in the market for the service. This is the outreach portion of prospecting.

It's a very simple concept. If you know someone at a company personally, then (a) you're more likely to find out when that company is looking for a new vendor, even if the search isn't publicly announced, and (b) you're more likely to be allowed to compete for the account.

In this kind of business, outreach efforts are designed to increase the number of people you know at companies that might eventually be looking for what your company sells.

"Outreach" is simply meeting strangers in a targeted way.

When I took my first agency new business job, at Levine, Huntley, my colleagues there gave me lots of advice on how I ought to begin making contacts with potential clients. Some thought I should first become an expert in some particular business field, such as banking, or health and beauty aids, or the automotive aftermarket. Then, when I called the advertisers in that industry, or wrote to them, they would be impressed by my knowledge and insight. They'd be more likely to trust their business to us.

The problem with this approach, in my mind, was that

no matter how much of an expert I could become in a week or two, or even in two or three months, I was never going to know as much or have quite the same perspective as someone who's worked in a particular business for a good part of his professional life. Moreover, it was clear to me that no one whose account was worth having was going to turn it immediately over to an advertising executive who writes him a letter or calls him up on the phone, no matter how impressed he is with the ad agency's insight. So I just didn't think becoming an overnight "expert" in a series of business categories was a winning strategy for prospecting.

Also, if I did it this way, I knew it would take me too long to put protons in my vat.

I wanted prospects. *Lots* of prospects. Right away. So my strategy was to call people cold without knowing much about them at all, except maybe their name and the kind of business they were in. Then I'd rely on my wits to make small talk and try to get them to tell me something about how they saw their own issues and problems.

Since that was my strategy, there was no reason not to go alphabetically through a directory of advertising clients. Except if I started in the A's and the B's, my colleagues would soon figure out what I was doing. They'd know my method was alphabetical and unscientific.

So I started in the L's, with companies like Lanier and

Levelor blinds, and so forth. After about a year of this, our very first new business client, derived from my prospecting efforts, was Management Science America (now part of D&B)—an "M" company, one of my first hundred or so contacts.

Now, I certainly didn't totally confine my prospecting to an alphabetical list of companies from a directory. I would contact other people too. If I read an article in the paper or in a trade magazine that seemed to indicate that such and such a client might be in the market for a new agency within a few weeks or months, I would be sure to call him and try to make a contact, for instance. But the directory was my primary vehicle—it was simply the most comprehensive source of protons.

 Cold-Calling

One way to prospect is by making cold calls, as I did in the advertising business—phoning companies one at a time, and trying to reach the person at each one who has authority over the contract you want.

I'm not really talking about telemarketing here. I don't believe hiring a telemarketer to make hundreds or thousands of outbound phone calls on behalf of a professional service is a very productive way to get business. Certainly telemarketing is neither appropriate nor effective for a law firm or an investment bank, for instance, and it's not for most ad agencies either.

Nor do I think fooling the prospect into taking your call is a very useful way to run an outreach program—not if your goal is to establish a network of contacts, each of which might be helpful to you only months or years from now. I once heard a motivational sales talk in which the speaker claimed she could get anyone anywhere to take her call simply by fooling the person into believing she was really just an old friend. If she were trying to reach, say, Lee Iacocca, she would call his office and ask his assistant briefly whether "Lee" was in, saying only to tell him "Kathy" was on the phone. The typical assistant routinely asks for a number to call back, even if her boss probably already has it somewhere, and Kathy would wait until the assistant asked before giving her the number—as if her good friend "Lee" already had it. If the assistant probed at all, Kathy would get "interrupted" on her end, have to get off the line right away, and please just tell Lee to call when he gets the chance. Then Lee does it, because he, too, thinks this Kathy must be someone he knows, or should remember.

This is a form of what I call "slash and burn" telemarketing. If you have a large number of prospects and are selling a one-time-purchase item with a high sticker, I suppose you can afford to irritate ninety-nine prospects to make one good sale. (That is, in fact, exactly how this particular motivational speaker summed up her telemarketing technique.) But it really is like slash-and-burn agriculture. You have to start with a whole lot of jungle to be able to survive as a slash-and-burn culture for even a single generation. And although in some situations it might, technically, make business sense, my opinion about fooling someone into taking a call is different. I think it stinks, and I hate it when people do it to me.

In my own theory of prospecting, it really doesn't make business sense either. The goal of a prospecting outreach program in my business has always been to make contact with someone now, in order to keep up with him informally for whatever time it takes before his company's account goes up for grabs. At that point, *if* he's still on friendly terms with me, then I have a real advantage.

Yes, you want to put as many "protons" in your vat as possible, but you also have to *keep* them in there! And the simple truth is you can get through to a business executive on the phone in lots of friendly ways.

If you have a list of people whose fingers are on the triggers of the budgets you'd like to compete for, there's certainly no harm in picking up the phone and trying to reach them one at a time, provided you remember your primary goal: planting seeds that will grow, over time, into a healthy crop of prospects. One out of every ten calls or so, you're going to catch someone, especially if you call early in the morning, late in the day, or during the lunch hour. These are the times when the secretary's usually not in, the executive's phone isn't covered, and sometimes he or she will pick it up in person.

Getting Past the Screener

The screener, who is usually a secretary or personal assistant, can certainly be an obstacle. That's her job, to insulate her boss from having to talk to solicitors.

The first rule for getting past a screener is never to deceive her. Make it a point to be totally honest with her about why you want to talk to her boss.

"I want to talk to him about my company." Or "I want to talk to him about his company." Or "I want to invite him to a meeting we're going to have" or to a presentation at such and such a city. Or "I want to put him on the mailing list for a marketing newsletter."

The screener will usually say, "I can handle that for him" or "Put it in a letter first." Always respond, "I'd be glad to send him a letter, but then may I talk to him on the phone?"

Be persistent, call back exactly at the time the screener recommends, and always respect the interests of the prospect you're trying to reach—her boss. In most cases it's in the prospect's own interest to have some kind of contact with you anyway. Sooner or later, at least if you've chosen your prospect well, he or she is likely to have some kind of responsibility for putting a list of contenders together, or for evaluating a set of vendors. Most such executives have a legitimate need to stay in touch with your industry.

Once you've established contact with a prospect, the effectiveness of your own program with that prospect will at least partly be a function of how well *you* serve the prospect's interests even *before* his business goes up for review (see Chapter Twenty-three).

The second rule is to make the screener your ally— even your friend. Chances are, if you really try to talk to her boss you'll be calling his office several times before successfully making a connection, if you ever do. Usually, you'll be speaking with the screener each time. So remember her name (make a note of it) and be friendly.

I've had secretaries I've befriended tell me when they're going to be away from the office for half an hour, and they expect their boss to be answering the phone on his own. That way the secretary can help me without really betraying her boss. She's still doing her job. She knows he's going to answer the phone anyway while she's away. All she's doing is giving me a little tip.

Actually, I've made great friends with some of the screeners I've talked to over the years. For example, it took me a very long time to reach the president of Paddington Corporation, the liquor importer. The only person I talked to for several weeks' worth of phoning was Mindy, his assistant. Naturally, she and I eventually became great telephone buddies.

Mindy helped me try to reach her boss. She knew why I was calling, and she knew her job was to screen her boss from having to deal with calls like mine. But after helping him dodge them for so long, and knowing I was just trying to have a single, ordinary, simple conversation, she felt guilty. She apologized to me more than once for her boss's inaccessibility, which seemed to her almost rude.

Finally, with Mindy's help I did reach him, we had a nice conversation, and I started sending him a few items of interest. He actually became quite interested in our agency, eventually giving us a shot at competing for a couple of his brands. (Unfortunately, by the time we were given this opportunity we had to turn it down, because we had landed some conflicting Seagram products in the interim!) Two or three years after this I left Levine, Huntley to work for Lintas. When I was making the rounds and being introduced to everyone, I met Mindy personally.

She had left Paddington and taken a job as the personal assistant to Lintas's creative director, Frank.

One advantage of making a screener your friend is that you can get an immense amount of very useful nonpublic information. Make it a practice, for instance, to ask a friendly screener a lot about her boss. I usually ask her what kind of furniture he or she has in the office, and what kind of pictures are up on the walls. How does her boss dress? What kind of meetings does he go to? Does he like to be entertained?

Making "Voice Contact"

My goal in every cold call is to have a conversational interchange with the executive I'm trying to reach. If I can just *converse* with this individual, then I can write her letters in the future that begin with the salutation "Dear Ann," rather than "Dear Ms. Jackson." I can send her news items on her industry, with personal notes referring back to our conversation. I can handwrite little postscripts on letters I send her. If we can become speaking acquaintances, I can call her when her account goes into review and she'll talk to me. But most important, if I can have a conversation with a prospect, I can learn things about how to win that prospect's business later.

Lots of people in the advertising business make cold calls in order to tell people about their agency. But if your prospecting objective is to make a personal contact that can be useful later—maybe much later—in getting into the competition for a particular company's business, then calling people up to tell them about your firm is not very productive.

The reason you should *call* someone (as opposed to writing them, for instance) is not so you can talk to them, but so they can talk to *you*. You want a prospect to tell you what she's looking for. What she really wants. What she's like. And be sure to take notes. Be organized, because the truth is that prospecting is strictly a numbers business.

When I place a call to someone, I obviously have to have an immediate objective in mind for the conversation. And when the screener asks me why I want to speak with her boss, I can hardly say I just want to "make voice contact," although in most cases that really is ninety percent of the goal. So I always have an immediate message, or need for conversation—inviting him to a presentation, talking with him about the widget industry's financial future, or just "telling him about my firm."

Once I make voice contact, however, what I really want more than anything is for the prospect to talk to me about his firm, about his issues, his problems. I want him to tell me as much as he feels comfortable telling me—and not just about his company, but about himself, his ambitions, his history.

It was through conversations with prospects that I first began visualizing how a person responds to different suggestions. When you get somebody on the phone the first time, you don't know what she looks like. You don't know whether she's old or young or heavyset, rigid or flexible or creative. There are lots and lots of variables. So I find myself trying to look for clues in the conversation, and the first clue I look for is whether this particular prospect is a make-me-rich or a make-me-famous type.

Once I've talked with someone on the phone or in person, I want to be sure she never forgets the fact that we've actually talked with each other. I have to keep this newly contacted prospect "warm" until whatever time her company's account goes into review. This can mean years of prospect "cultivation," so what I think about is not only putting as many protons in the vat as possible, but keeping them there too.

Cultivating these prospects over the months or years it takes to bring in an account is the subject of Chapter Twenty-three.

▼ Numbers Game

Early on in my career I did some simple estimates and calculations to help myself understand the economics of prospecting:

1. The typical advertising account had a life of five to seven years, according to a trade press article on the subject.

2. There were perhaps six hundred accounts in the entire country which were big enough—but not too big—for my firm. (I estimated this by sampling twenty or thirty pages from a directory, then projecting the results.) Most of these accounts were in advertising budgets in the range of $10 to 20 million, making them worth $1 to 3 million in annual revenue for my firm.

3. This meant that every year there were about one hundred reviews we would like to participate in, if we could—about two a week, although they seemed to come in groups.

4. My firm was already being invited into about ten reviews a year. These were the "over the tran-

som" contests we had always relied on to win new accounts.

5. I estimated that even if we didn't already know someone at a prospect company, when the company announced its review we still had perhaps a five percent chance of getting into the pitch. That's about what my experience indicated, anyway.

6. Thus, we were already being invited into about ten reviews a year, and we could probably squeeze into another four or five just by crashing the gate. So we would be getting fourteen or fifteen pitch opportunities a year with no prospecting at all —about fifteen percent of the reviews that were out there. We were not able to compete, in other words, in eighty-five percent of the reviews we would like to have competed in.

7. Then I made the conservative assumption that if we actually *knew* someone at a prospect company when they announced their review—if we had previously contacted someone influential and then kept in touch over the years—we would have at least a fifty percent chance of getting into that company's review when it happened. We would be more likely to get invited to participate in a review organized by a company where we were already

known to the organizers, and we would be more likely to be able to wangle a spot in such a review even if we weren't originally invited.

8. Thus, for every hundred voice-contacts in my program—for every hundred protons in the vat— we would be able to get into about seven more reviews per year.

▼▼

100 contacts ÷ 6 years average life of account = 16 reviews per year, among the contacts
16 reviews × 85% = 13.6 reviews we wouldn't have gotten into
13.6 reviews × 50% = 7 more reviews we could get into if we knew someone

▼▼

9. Next, with a little experience I figured I could actually get two to three new contacts per full day of prospecting effort.

10. So, if I allocated just one half my time and effort to prospecting (with the other half consumed by pitching), I figured I could make voice contact with twenty to twenty-five desirable new prospects per month—maybe two hundred per year.

11. Thus, by allocating just fifty percent of my time to prospecting—if I stayed with it and didn't let up—I could double the rate at which we were getting into reviews within a year.

12. If we won, on average, about twenty percent of the reviews we got into, then with no prospecting effort at all we would still be getting maybe three pieces of business a year. This was, in fact, about what the agency was doing, year in and year out. But after one year of half-time prospecting, we would be winning an *additional* three accounts per year.

13. The best part: If I kept prospecting half-time, at the end of the second year we would have added *another* two hundred prospects to the list, on top of the first year's two hundred. So we ought to win *six* new accounts that year that we wouldn't have won without prospecting, and so on and so on. This would continue for as long as I could comfortably manage the number of protons we were putting into the vat, or until we actually knew someone personally at every one of the six hundred or so prospect companies in our market.

Some Tips for a Face-to-Face Meeting

When you are fortunate enough to be able to schedule a face-to-face meeting with a prospect you haven't yet met, follow these steps:

1. Never call to confirm your meeting once it's set up. Obviously, calling will just give the prospect an opportunity to reconsider whether he has the time or inclination to meet at all. The worst thing that can happen if you don't call to confirm a meeting is really the best thing for you—the prospect stands you up because he forgets about it. Now he really owes you one. The only exception might be if you are traveling a distance by air to meet. If the meeting is out of town, then *not* calling might be seen as a little silly on your part.

2. If it's a meal or other entertainment, don't be the first to bring up business. The prospect will bring the subject up eventually. He'll have to, or he'll leave feeling guilty. And if you let the prospect bring up the subject, you'll get an insight into what aspects of your business he sees as the most important.

3. Get the prospect to do all the talking you can. Sometimes you won't have to say much at all. If you're invited to explain your firm, do so briefly and modestly. Tell the prospect you'll follow up with a brochure, or hand him one on the spot. But don't read its contents to him.

4. Remember what the prospect says. Be an active listener, take notes if it's not inappropriate, and immediately after your meeting go back to your office and dictate or type out as detailed an account as you possibly can, for your file. Include any key words you picked up, any nuances, and *don't forget personal information* if any came up.

5. Don't sell. Period. Don't give the prospect a hard sell, and don't give him a soft sell. Remember: Your goal is to get this contact into your prospect management system, and keep him warm until an opportunity presents itself. You can't create the opportunity simply by telling him how great your firm is, so don't try. Instead, concentrate on being a great listener, and getting the prospect to tell you more and more and more.

Don Peppers

Be a "Mystery Shopper"

In this book I cover lots of things you can do to make sure you develop as many prospects as possible. Follow my suggestions and you're going to make more and more contacts with people you don't know now. You're going to work on sustaining productive relationships with those you do know. But it's a lot of work. Every new contact is a hard-won asset for your firm.

So, while you are launching this all-out effort to gain new contacts, why not take a few minutes every week to make sure your company is doing the most basic things right with "over the transom" business? You can't simply assume they will be done right all the time, without feedback.

Play "mystery shopper" with your own firm. Restaurant chains and department stores hire people to patronize their own establishments and note how the service was. A mystery shopper might go into a fast-food restaurant, make some special request, and then make notes regarding how fast and how effectively the restaurant responds.

You should do the same. Make calls to various places in your firm, pretend you are a potential new client trying to find out where to send an RFP inquiry, or how to get a sample of the firm's work. See what happens.

Write a letter like that to your firm, addressing it to no one in particular, and see how long it takes for the letter to arrive on the desk of the business-development officer and generate action. Send the letter to different divisions, or call different offices.

Chapter 22
▼▼▼▼▼▼

Other Ways to Reach Out

There are many other ways to make voice contact with someone you don't know right now but whom you'd like to get to know. In the old days, it was a matter of joining the right clubs, or golfing on the right courses. I suppose that's still one way to meet people in some circles, but frankly, I'm not a golfer.

I do know, however, that cold-calling can be supplemented with a large variety of innovative ways to meet people. Somewhat like a single man or woman on the hunt for potentially compatible mates, you have to sit down, think it out scientifically, and then evaluate all the options you face in the cold light of realism. Go where your prospects are. Create reasons for them to come to where you are. And don't overlook any opportunities that might already be right under your nose.

Start with Your Current Inventory

If your goal is to have as many protons in the vat as possible, then the first place to look is in the vat. How many prospects do you already know? You might be surprised at the answer. There are several sources of prospects available to you already, some of which you might not have tapped.

1. Current employees. Go through your company and take an inventory of every executive's business card file and address book (with his or her permission, of course!). Then interview these executives with respect to past employers, past client contacts, association meetings, current and former colleagues, and so forth.

For every live prospect identified in this manner, be sure to ask the executive if the name of this prospect reminds him or her of any *other* prospects, even at the same organization. Just because you have one contact at a company doesn't mean you don't want a dozen. Take the dozen whenever you can get it.

2. Current clients and customers. Now look carefully at your list of current clients and customers. If you have good, healthy relationships with your customers, you'll be able to perform practically the same kind of inventory with their files as you do with the address books and files of your own executives. Account executives in charge of individual client contacts should be equipped with a questionnaire to probe current client colleagues at noncompetitive companies, as well as former acquaintances, and so forth.

Every discussion of fee and services should involve a tail-end request by you for more referrals. At various times, you've probably given a lot of money back to clients, compared to what you wanted to charge—what you asked for in the beginning. Every time you do this, you ought to ask for some help on the new-business front. Your customers aren't blind to your need. They're in business too. They know what the score is, and if they like what you're doing for them, they'll usually exert some effort on your behalf. It doesn't cost them anything, right?

3. Converting losers into potential winners. Dig through the files that exist on every past competition and pitch your firm has participated in. Anyone whose business you don't win today should become a prospect tomorrow. So talk to the current business-development people, dig through the files, and produce the names of the people who've thought about your firm already, at one time or another. Go back as much as twenty-four months—more if you have some special reason to think the executive involved might remember you fondly.

Also, put in place now an *automatic* system for ensuring that the executives on the prospect side of losing pitches get treated as follow-ups for future pitches. You want all the names of executives involved in every such pitch to go into your prospect file. By ensuring that you don't lose contact initially, you can be sure you'll stay in touch with them over the long term—until the next opportunity to pitch.

In the advertising business, while the average account stays at one agency for five to seven years, there are a large number of agency marriages that come undone before the first year is out. So don't burn bridges, no matter how off the mark a prospect's judgment might seem to you when a competitor is chosen.

Conference and Trade Show Blitzes

Once you've dug through all your own possible sources, why not simply travel to where prospects are congregating?

In every industry there are trade shows, conferences, conventions, meetings. If your goal is to meet prospects, a conference is one place to do it easily. My advice is go to a conference with enough executives—three or maybe five —so that you're prepared to take in *every* session. Exchange cards with the people sitting next to you, go up after each presentation and exchange cards with the speaker or panel members, and mingle at the cocktail hours.

Especially if you've zeroed in on one or two particular industries, catch the trade shows and conferences in those industries. Get an executive at your firm invited to speak at some of these conferences. It's really not hard. *Most* of the speakers at a trade conference are there only because they want to generate leads for their business.

When you return home with piles of business cards, be sure to send brief follow-up notes to everyone. It's important to document your relationship with people you just met so they'll remember you better, and be more willing to accept your phone call at a later time. I suggest sending a follow-up note of three or four sentences only, with a personally handwritten P.S. at the end that might remind the person where you were when you met and talked, what session you were taking in together, or something like that. Then, within a month, find another reason to send more correspondence—maybe a copy of your brochure for your new acquaintance's file, or a news article he or she might find of interest. Don't do it all at once. Spread it out.

If you have an opportunity to speak at a trade conference, be sure to allude to a more detailed study or report during your presentation. Make a specific reference, but be sure you don't have time to go into all the particulars. It doesn't hurt to have two or three such references in your speech, to different reports or studies on related topics. Without being blatant about it, what you want is for the members of the audience to have a reason to come up later and ask you to mail them a copy of some document that piqued their interest. You want business cards. Addresses. Phone numbers.

Also, be careful not to *sell* at a conference presentation. You're already selling just by being there—by being a smiling, commanding, knowledgeable presence. Don't contaminate the otherwise objective credibility of your message with a crass selling appeal.

Don Peppers

"Door Opener" Presentations

The "door opener" is one of my absolute favorite prospecting outreach techniques, because it's so high-ground. And it's so *easy*.

A good door opener should be a presentation about a topic that's unusual or unique, but of general business interest. If you're in the ad business, for instance, it could be a presentation on the impact of kids' environmental attitudes on the sale of products to their parents. Or it could be a point of view on the impact of new, interactive media on the dynamics of mass marketing and communications. In any case, the presentation has to be on a subject any one of your prospects, in nearly any business, will find somewhat appealing, and about which he might like to know more.

Your goal is to use this presentation to open doors at companies where you'd like to meet the executives. This means never target a door opener to a particular prospect's business. In most cases, even targeting a door opener to a particular industry is not wise—unless it's a very broad industry, with a lot of competitors.

This may sound odd, but think about it for a minute.

First, no matter how good you are, your insight about a particular company or industry is unlikely to be impressive unless you spend thousands of dollars and months of effort to do the research.

But second, not only will this be costly for you, but the prospect is likely to find it downright threatening. Go into a company with which you have no current relationship and unveil a highly specific presentation, making recommendations for their business, and the executives at this firm are less likely to be grateful than argumentative and defensive. It's human nature, so you might as well not fight it.

Here are the rules for maximizing the benefits of creating a door opener and using it to gather business cards:

- *Offer the presentation in person only.* Be sure it's not available in written or video form. Period, no exceptions. You can and should make handouts to accompany the presentation, but it shouldn't be too easy to get the story just from the handout.
- *Get a news article written about your presentation in a trade publication.* Although you'd welcome the publicity such a news article might generate, that's not really your primary goal. What you want is to have a reporter's coverage in print so you can use it to demonstrate the credibility of your presentation when you mail out invitations to

prospects. To generate a reporter's interest, you need at least one or two interesting or unusual conclusions or turns of phrase. If you think you have them, there are a couple of ways to get a story:

a. Find a meeting, conference, or suitable setting in which to make the first presentation. A convention will do, even if it's for your own industry. Conferences like this are often covered by trade reporters, so invite some to your session. If you don't succeed in getting an article this way, then:

b. Invite a friendly trade press reporter to a private showing of the presentation and give her an exclusive on it. This makes it more likely she'll write a story.

■ *Once the story has been published, clip it out and make copies.* Then send out letters to executives from your prospect organization and say, "We did this presentation and here's what so and so said about it from *Ad Age* or from *Ohio Lawyer.* If you'd like, we'll come to your offices, at no charge to you, and make the presentation."

When I was at Lintas we got an opportunity to speak at the American Advertising Federation convention on "the future of media." This was in the late 1980s, when interactivity was just beginning to be talked about seriously, and cable systems were starting to discuss three hundred-channel systems.

The American Advertising Federation is an organization that includes executives from both ad agencies and advertisers—potential clients. Because the audience was likely to include a good number of prospects, I accepted the opportunity on behalf of our agency, and then talked to Lou, the media director, about giving it. He declined, saying the subject was already too picked over and threadbare to support an interesting speech. At that point, I had no choice but to do the presentation myself, and while I was preparing for it I learned more about interactivity and media than I thought there was to know.

Once I gave the speech, it was clear I'd hit a soft spot with the audience. A good number of people came up afterward for copies of the slides I'd used, and months later I was still getting invitations to repeat the speech at various luncheon and dinner meetings. But the main use for this slide show and talk, as I saw it, would be to get ourselves invited in to business organizations where Lintas was unknown. I saw it as a terrific door opener.

To lend credibility to it, I got Lintas's director of research as well as the media director (the same one who originally turned down the opportunity) to join me in an interview by the advertising columnist at *The New York Times*. The reporter wanted to write a story on the fractionalization of media, and I told him we'd give an exclusive on our fairly unique perspective if he wanted it. (If this columnist had not wanted to do the article, our next stop was *Advertising Age,* where a friendly reporter had already asked me some questions indicating his interest in a similar topic.)

Sure enough, an article soon appeared in the paper discussing the controversial points raised in our presentation. So I had the article copied and began using the presentation as a serious door opener. On the strength of this presentation, Lintas was able to generate meetings with a number of companies where we really didn't know anyone to begin with, including McDonald's, Nintendo, Sara Lee, and other blue chip firms. At each of these meetings, we picked up five, ten, sometimes twenty business cards —each now a prospect for us to cultivate and grow.

This particular door opener became so important to me as a topic that I later collaborated on a book about it, *The One to One Future: Building Relationships One Customer at a Time,* which *Business Week* termed "one of the bibles of the new marketing." My whole consulting business is now oriented around new, one-to-one marketing strategies. But it started simply as a way to get in to see people I didn't know, at companies I wanted to do business with someday.

Use an ''Event'' to Draw Attendance

Another favorite tactic of mine is to draw prospects to an event that my firm stages. At Lintas, we rented a hotel ballroom in New York for half a day and staged what we called Lintas Future Day. Our agenda was to discuss the future of marketing. Because we were trying to position ourselves not just as a large advertising agency, but as an integrated communications company—experts in coordinating advertising with sales promotion, direct mail, and a number of other "below the line" promotional activities— Lintas Future Day would emphasize the blurring distinction among these types of promotion.

We invited Chris Whittle to speak, and he came for free (he wanted an audience too). We hired Nicholas Negroponte to give the keynote address. Negroponte, a brilliant speaker, heads MIT's media lab, and was recommended to us by his agent, the Leigh Bureau. We had to pay a five-figure speaking fee to book him.

We promoted our event with advertising in trade magazines and direct mail to prospect companies. We charged admission, for a couple of reasons. Obviously, we wanted to help liquidate our costs. But we also wanted to set a "value" on the event. We had a list of a hundred or so prime prospect executives to whom we sent letters offering *complimentary* admissions to the event. We didn't tell them the main purpose of the gathering was to gain their attendance in the first place. Our primary overall goal was to meet these prospects personally and talk with them briefly at the event or, if we already knew them, to improve their opinion of Lintas and its capabilities.

Because we advertised the event and charged admission, we allowed executives from competitive agencies to attend. A lot of them actually bought tickets and showed up. Why? Because we were comping their clients, that's why. Our little joke was that our competitors were welcome to attend Lintas Future Day if they wanted to, and their clients could even come free.

We also comped large delegations from most of our own clients, so in the end almost the only attendees who actually paid to come were from competitive agencies. Of the three hundred or so who attended the half-day event, enough paid the admission price to liquidate about eighty percent of the cost.

You don't necessarily have to stage your own event to attract prospects, like we did with Lintas Future Day. You could also hire the event out. Contract with someone else to put on a presentation that you "sponsor." Invite your own prospects.

One of my consulting firm's current clients is a company called Sky Alland. This company is in the customer-satisfaction business. They use thousands of telephone calls to survey recent car purchasers, house refinancers, and the like to probe for complaints or service problems. They maintain their own very sophisticated database, and feed back information to their clients on a daily basis. It's a well-organized version of "complaint discovery," something every serious relationship marketer must do. It's somewhat like mystery shopping.

One of the ways Sky Alland gets new clients is by staging events. They hire my firm to run a brief seminar on the nature of relationship marketing and the uses of new, interactive media in a particular industry—say, automobiles, or financial institutions. Then they publicize this event to potential clients. Admission is free, but by invitation only.

At one of the very first of these events, staged in Detroit for auto executives, one of the attendees turned out to be the executive in charge of relationship marketing for Oldsmobile's new Aurora. The Aurora was a few months away from being launched. On the basis of this staged event, and the follow-ups immediately afterward, Sky Alland was asked to bid on the Aurora's telephone program, and they won the contract—it turned into an immense piece of business.

Don Peppers

Write a Book

A few months after creating the door-opener presentation on new media and its impact on marketing, I met Martha Rogers at a talk I gave in Toledo and we began our collaboration on *The One to One Future.* We started working on the book in early 1990, and it was nearly four years before it actually appeared in print. A lot of the book was written, or at least researched, while I was still in the advertising business, working at Chiat/Day.

Martha and I knew of several companies whose views we wanted on the topic, and since I was the one most accustomed to calling people up out of the blue and asking them for things, I did most of the calling.

Guess what I found out? If you call someone and tell him you're working on a book and would like to do an interview, you almost always get through. It worked like a charm. It was the single best tactic I'd ever seen when it came to getting through to prospects!

It turned out that there were a lot of Chiat/Day prospects I found a reason to interview for our book. We hadn't even had a proposal accepted by a publisher yet, but I had no trouble whatsoever in getting in to see a wide variety of very valuable potential clients. I would call up, leave a message about my intent with the assistant, and then more often than not the assistant would call me back to schedule a convenient time to meet!

Like a good journalist, I taped each interview, and the discussions really were helpful in putting our book together. But following up an interview, I put the prospect I'd been in to see into our system, and began the long, slow "prospect cultivation" process.

How to Burn Bridges

Some people love to burn bridges. As self-destructive as it is, burning bridges is a constant activity, practiced by many of the best and brightest business executives—especially highly successful, entrepreneurial ones.

If you want to burn more bridges with colleagues, business associates, and potential future customers, and you want to burn them to a totally unsalvageable crisp, then follow these simple guidelines:

1. Always talk about yourself or your firm. Don't waste time discussing the prospect.

2. Be openly disparaging of all your competitors, especially your prospect's current vendor.

3. Call a prospective client on the phone, fawn over his business, wax eloquent about how carefully your firm has followed his, and how interested you've always been in his account. Then, when he doesn't launch a review after all, don't contact him again—don't follow up by phone, don't write any letters or notes to him, nothing. Don't waste any time on him at all until the next time there's a rumor he might be looking.

4. When you are defeated for a piece of business:

  a. Blame everyone but yourself.
  b. Blame the client if at all possible.
  c. Argue with the client to convince him he's made a wrong decision.
  d. Try to humiliate or threaten your victorious competitor.

Burned Bridges I Have Witnessed

When New York Air finally did give Levine, Hunt-ley their advertising account, they notified their current agency, Bloom, of the switch, whereupon Bloom's CEO, Bob Bloom, mailed an absolutely sizzling letter of complaint to Frank Lorenzo. If I remember it correctly, the letter accused the com-pany's executives at New York Air of double-deal-ing, lying, failing to watch out for Mr. Lorenzo's interests in New York, and general moral turpitude.

It was quite a letter, because Frank forwarded it to his people at New York Air, and the New York Air executives made copies of it and sent one to us. Frank had scribbled a note at the top of the letter —something like "Is this guy out of control? Do we need to worry?"

I was very happy to get a copy of this note, be-cause I knew it was like an insurance policy for us. Getting any new relationship off to a healthy start is a difficult job, and frequently advertising relation-ships sour within the first few weeks or months. Now I knew that New York Air could not go back.

If our relationship soured, they would either have to work hard with us to fix it, or start all over again and find a totally new firm. They could no longer simply call Bloom up, confess a mistake, and return.

When I began doing new-business work for Chiat/Day I learned that the agency had burned an extraordinary number of bridges in its twenty-year history. This was in spite of the fact that Chiat/Day had always been right out on the cutting edge of innovation and creativity. When I joined them and began making prospect contacts, I found about a one-third chance that any individual prospect was already angry at Chiat, for one reason or another.

Chiat/Day has always had a reputation for arrogance in the industry. It is a well-deserved reputation, but it's also quite understandable. Since about 1980, Chiat/Day has stood literally head and shoulders above the rest of the industry when it comes to creative executions. They've done everything from the famous "1984" commercial that launched the Apple Macintosh, to the Eveready bunny, and many other famous (and sometimes infamous) commercials in between.

The problem I found when I arrived at Chiat/Day was that this arrogance had burned many bridges. Sometimes Chiat executives came across in a new-business presentation as condescending or self-righteous. Other times, if a client invited Chiat to pitch its account but then gave the account to another agency, Chiat's executives were publicly dismissive. Obviously, a more intelligent client would have chosen Chiat/Day, right?

Beating a Path to Sara Lee

At Levine, Huntley, I could make all the prospecting calls myself. But at Lintas, a much larger agency, I had to organize coworkers' efforts. That's when I began visualizing the benefits of collaborating with other people in terms of *contact paths.*

It's simple math, really. If you have only one person at your company who has a relationship with someone at the prospect firm, then you have one contact path between your company and the prospect.

Don Peppers

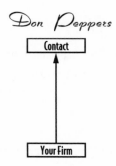

One Possible Contact Path

If you have two people calling two prospect executives, then by cross-selling one against the other you actually have four possible contact paths.

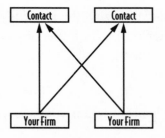

Four Possible Contact Paths

Increase it to three, and you'll have nine contact paths into the prospect.

And so it goes, increasing exponentially.

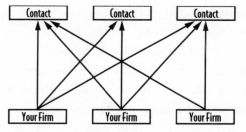

Nine Possible Contact Paths

Open every contact path you can. But then you must manage communication very carefully. The principal contact path should be maintained between the two executives, at your firm and the prospect's, who enjoy the best relationship. If your own executive leaves your firm, however, you'll have other contact paths to fall back on.

A $100-Million Set of Contact Paths

When Lintas was trying to position itself as an integrated marketing firm that could deliver more than just advertising, we targeted Sara Lee as one of our top prospects. We wanted to work on their meat accounts, worth some $100 million in total. The problem was that each brand developed its own advertising separately, which meant separate reviews and a chaotic rather than integrated marketing effort. But we wanted the whole business, and we felt sooner or later Sara Lee would want an integrated, coordinated program itself.

At that time Lintas had a tactical marketing program run by Sheila. She would develop relationships with numerous stores in one city and then put together a package for the manufacturer that would enable them to sell more products. Her projects were virtually turnkey to the manufacturer. Although it was time-consuming work for her staff, manufacturers found these programs irresistible.

So we decided to sic Sheila on a number of Sara Lee's different brands. Pretty soon we had six different tactical marketing projects going within different areas of the company. In fact, we had so many different contact paths into the organization that we knew what they were planning before the chief operating officer read his subordinates' reports.

After more than a year of this, Sara Lee announced they were going to have a review for the entire meat business, all at once. They had decided to integrate all their different advertising programs into one overall effort. All the agencies they had been working with at various divisions were going to compete, and so were we. Each of our competitors was highly knowledgeable about the division it had been working with, but none of them had anywhere near as many links into the bigger organization as we did.

After a lengthy review, we won the business. It was a $100-million victory.

Chapter 23

▼▼▼▼▼▼

Prospect Management: Cultivating the Crop

If an outreach program is something like planting seeds, the prospect management process is crop cultivation. After planting as many seeds as you can, you have to wait for them to mature, but your results will always be better if you help the crop along—watering, nurturing the plants, putting the right amount of nutrient in the ground, giving your plants whatever they need to grow. The more a plant grows, the more valuable it becomes to you, even though it might not be ready to harvest yet.

The goal of a prospect management program is to stay in every prospect's "line of sight" as long as possible, unobtrusively and cost-effectively—to keep the relationship between you and the prospect growing. Eight months, or eight years, from when you first meet someone or talk to him on the phone, you want him to remember you well enough to give your firm some consideration when he chooses a new vendor. At the very minimum, you want him to take your phone call at a time when he probably won't be taking very many.

It's a lot of work to manage prospect relationships in such a way that the prospect isn't overwhelmed and annoyed, but doesn't forget you either. If your idea of prospect communication is to send out periodic examples of your company's work, or press clippings on your firm's kudos and accomplishments, then you might as well save the postage money. Instead, concentrate on providing something of value to the prospect, on a regular basis. It's the easiest way to keep a prospect on the front burner with you.

We live in an information flood. So why not serve the prospect's interests by sifting some of this information and condensing it, for instance? Or send out easy-to-digest competitive analyses and reports. Once you have a hundred, or five hundred, prospects under management— people you know by first name—I would suggest creating a newsletter, or something similar. The point is to have some excuse for sending personal notes to the people in your database on a regular basis. A newsletter, if it's done right, is a good vehicle for that.

Don Peppers

If you succeed in recruiting other executives at your firm into the prospecting outreach process, inventorying their card files, sending them on conference blitzes, and maybe even getting a few of them to make cold calls on behalf of the firm, then each of these executives will soon have his or her own "first-name list" of voice-contact prospects. An executive with a first-name list should be the signatory on any piece of correspondence that goes to the contacts on his list. He is the "sponsor" for each of the contacts on his own first-name list.

A significant benefit of cross-selling one contact path against another is that it will have the effect of tying your organization more tightly together. When the direct mail subsidiary exchanges prospect information with the sales promotion division, or when the Houston regional headquarters exchanges information with the Denver field office, they can't help but become more closely tied to each other.

The contents of your newsletter should be of general interest to your current and potential customers. It shouldn't be an ad for you, at least not in the conventional sense. So I'm not talking about sending out a newsletter with articles that say "here's what's great at ABC agency," or "here's what's cooking at the XYZ architectural firm." I'm talking about a newsletter that covers subjects of general interest to the people who have their fingers on the budget triggers—articles a person on your prospect list is likely to consider worthwhile reading.

Depending on the type of newsletter you create, it should be mailed out three to six times a year to all the prospects you've managed to meet. And it should be mailed with a cover letter or some other personal communication from the contact's sponsor—from you, if you're the one who knows the prospect personally, or from the executive at your firm who does know him.

When I arrived at Lintas, the agency's research people were putting out a six-page newsletter every two to three months. The publication, which was called *Staying Relevant,* consisted almost entirely of condensed articles from other publications. These articles were frequently centered around a loosely structured theme, dealing with some aspect of marketing. It was a thoroughly professional job. *Staying Relevant* was what I call "airplane reading"—the kind of reading that is interesting and easy to scan, that you might slip into your briefcase in order to fill a spare ten or twenty minutes while you're sitting on a taxiway.

The only problem was, Lintas's method for sending this newsletter out was not at all helpful when it came to keeping prospects "warm." In fact, it was actually harmful. The agency was simply sending this newsletter to a cold roster of prospects whose names and titles had been bought from a mailing list company somewhere. Every letter began "Dear Mr.____" or "Dear Ms.____," and had a facsimile signature from our agency chairman. It was on the chairman's letterhead. But I would bet not one in fifty of the recipients of this letter actually thought the chairman read or signed the letter. It was, in fact, nothing more than an expensive piece of junk mail.

But it was even worse than that. Simply scanning through the list of addressees revealed a number of people who were already known personally to one or more executives at Lintas. Some were executives who had even been in to see the agency on various occasions in the past (ex-clients, participants in unsuccessful past reviews, and so forth). In other words, even though executives at our agency had personal contacts whose names happened to be on this purchased list, these contacts still received the newsletter as if it were junk mail from the agency chairman—just as if they were anonymous "targets" in a pile. So not only were we overlooking a great opportunity to keep all our personal contacts "warm" with a worthwhile occasional mailing, we were actually telling many of them we *didn't care.* They *weren't* special.

To deal with this problem, we eliminated the "cold" mailing altogether, and set in place a policy that no prospect would get mailed a *Staying Relevant* unless someone at Lintas knew the prospect by first name. That Lintas executive, designated as the prospect's sponsor, was responsible for approving any correspondence or other communication sent to the prospect. It was the same way we handled current clients. No client service business would send mass-produced memos or letters to its current clients without the active participation of the account directors, right?

The rule we put in place was that every prospect on our mailing list had to be an actual personal voice contact of some kind, which meant each had to have a sponsor who would sign the cover letter personally. We then went through every Lintas executive's card file and address book, making sure we had inventoried all the prospects we already knew. The typical Lintas sponsor had a first-name list of twenty to fifty names, even before we began organizing a prospect outreach program.

Altogether, among the twenty or so key executives at the agency, we identified over five hundred separate, unduplicated prospect names—names of prospect executives already known personally by someone at the agency. After this thorough analysis of our own resources, it turned out that the *majority* of "cold" names who had been receiving junk mail letters from the agency chairman were actually "warm" contacts, already known to some senior executive somewhere in the Lintas organization!

Our business development department played "traffic

cop"—ensuring that no prospect had more than one sponsor, for instance, and making sure the newsletters to be mailed out were placed on the right sponsors' desks. (In any case—and there were many—in which a single contact was known by several sponsors, we "assigned" the sponsorship either to the most senior Lintas executive, or to the one we felt would do the best follow-up job, over time.)

We composed the cover letters and placed them on the sponsor's desk, so the only thing the sponsor had to do was sign each one and write a personal P.S. The hand-written postscript was not required in every case, but strongly recommended, and most newsletters did go out with one- or two-sentence, handwritten personal notes. In relatively few cases a sponsor would want a different cover letter altogether, and we accommodated him. With his own list of contacts, the sponsor has to be the one in charge.

Bragging Modestly

If our agency had something really important that was worth crowing about—something that we were doing that made us unique, or that our prospective clients ought to appreciate—then we had to find a creative way to talk about it. We never just sent ad slicks out in the mail. Lots of ad agencies do this, but I think it's pointless. It's funny that no agency would ever recommend this kind of a marketing campaign to its own clients, but many think nothing of sticking their most recent self-congratulatory achievements into envelopes and sending them out.

Instead, when you really have something to say that's newsworthy, but involves some accomplishment or achievement by your firm, find a way to send the news out with a creative device or benefit for the recipient.

For instance, when I was at Levine, Huntley we were breaking a very creative television ad campaign on the 1985 Super Bowl for New York Air. Because the airline competed against the Eastern Shuttle in Boston, Washington, and New York, the commercials were going to run only in those cities. A few weeks ahead of time I combed through the contact files and got a list of the two hundred or so prospects we knew by first name, and who lived in one of these cities. We knew, of course, that almost all the men, and a good portion of the women, would be tuned in.

So we sent each a regulation NFL football, delivered on the Wednesday morning prior to Super Bowl Sunday, with a letter that said, essentially, "Watch the Super Bowl for new commercials from New York Air." We felt a football, wrapped in a big box and delivered to the office, was something useful and interesting, without being offensive or exorbitant.

When we won the Perrier/Jouet advertising account from Seagram, the first thing I did was order several cases of the little champagne splits. Then we sent out a little split of champagne to our contacts, along with a letter announcing we'd won the account. I kept several cases of the splits to use in the prospect management program, whenever we sent out congratulatory notes.

Making "Opportunity" Contacts

In addition to sending out regular correspondence, perhaps accompanying a newsletter, you need to look thoroughly for any reasonable excuse to call or write a prospect. Keep in mind any ongoing contact program has the potential to annoy a prospect if it's carried to excess. The best way not to annoy is to find reasons to contact the prospect that are oriented around his or her own business success—not yours.

So be sure to pick up any mention of your first-name contacts in the trade press. The truth is, the most frequent mention of an executive by name in the press occurs when she leaves the company, gets fired, gets replaced, or earns a promotion. Occasionally there will be other news about her company, not mentioning her by name, but significant enough to warrant a personal communication anyway—such as when her company acquires another, or launches a high-profile new product.

That's why I kept the cases of Perrier-Jouet champagne —for the "good news" occasions that justified a personal contact with someone on my first-name list. I'd send her a letter with a little bottle of Perrier-Jouet saying congratulations, good work, or something else that didn't require any action or reply on the contact's part.

Ad agencies are big on sending out videotapes of their commercials. Many ad agencies send out commercials on 3/4-inch reels. These are professional, high-quality videotape reels with higher picture resolution and sharper definition than the more popular half-inch VHS reels you play on your home VCR. However, no one has a 3/4-inch tape player at home, and most advertising client executives have one only in the office, somewhere down the hall—if they happen to work at a big company.

When we won the Panasonic business, our job was to promote their VHS tapes. So it gave me a great excuse to send out a reel of our commercials without being obnoxiously self-congratulatory about it. We sent out 120-minute VHS tapes, with our commercials already recorded on

$\mathcal{D}on$ $\mathcal{P}eppers$

the first ten minutes or so. The attached letter said something like:

▼▼▼

Enjoy this Panasonic videotape in your home VCR with our compliments. If you're like me, your family's always scrambling to find a spare tape to record some movie that's just started on the television. The first ten minutes on this tape has a sampling of commercials produced by our agency, and since we sent you the tape, maybe you'd like to look at our commercials. But we didn't punch the tabs out, so feel free to record over our commercials any time, although we think you might find them entertaining by themselves.

▼▼▼

And don't forget your current customers! If you do send out videotapes, bottles of champagne, footballs, or anything else, be sure to send them to your current customers as well.

Keep It Simple

Meeting prospects, and then managing your relationships with each of them, is a time-consuming, detail-oriented task. You should computerize and automate as much of it as possible, not only to reduce the manual workload, but also to eliminate human error. Nothing should ever go into your permanent prospect address files, for instance without it having been checked twice to ensure perfect spelling, style, and grammar. That way you'll always be certain, if a name and title are in the permanent file, the name is spelled right and the title was checked.

To keep your prospect database fresh, no matter how many prospects you have in it, you should reverify every name, title, and address regularly. Charge someone in your organization with calling thirty-three percent of the prospects in your file every two months—or every three months, or every six months, depending on how carefully you want to maintain your database.

Because computer technology is developing so fast, there are any number of off-the-shelf contact-management programs today that can help manage this task. In the late 1980s, when we first installed a prospect-management system on our personal computers at Lintas, we spent something like $40,000 for the system, not counting some internal programming labor. The system included e-mail, and it had to connect our computers in New York and Detroit. Today I'm sure any business could buy a similarly capable system for perhaps $5000 in program licensing fees and network server equipment. And if you don't need the networking part, you can buy a PC-based contact manager for $100 or less.

Doing Favors

Never miss an opportunity to do a favor or perform an inexpensive service for a contact. If your prospect expresses an interest in getting a copy of some report or news article, get it. If he wants to get tickets to a hard-to-get-into play, get them for him from your corporate scalper. In most cases like this, you should charge the prospect what it cost you, particularly if it was expensive. To do less will look too much like a bribe.

My favorite tactic for winning allegiance is to offer a spare office and the use of a secretary to any contact of mine who loses his or her job. For most of my career I've worked in New York City. So even if a contact is let go from his company in Des Moines, he may well want access to a spare office in New York on occasion. Once or twice I've been taken up on the offer, but even when my contact never needs the office he will remember the generosity. Usually it costs me absolutely nothing but a five-minute phone call.

A good rule of thumb is that whenever you have a chance to do something for or on behalf of a prospect, do it. You want your prospect to be "in your debt" at the time his account goes up for review. Being in your debt will not obligate him to give you the business, but it will almost certainly mean he will go out of his way to ensure your firm gets an objective hearing.

Your Prospect Mailing Program: A "How-to" Guide

1. Publish a newsletter or document of general interest to your prospects.
- *Make it inexpensive to produce (could be desktop published)*
- *Find an "editor" internally who is capable*

- *Don't create the newsletter from scratch, but "borrow" its contents from other publications (with permission and attribution)*

2. Avoid using the mailing as a promotional vehicle to "sell" your firm to the people who receive the mailing.
- *No promotional literature from your firm*
- *No selling come-on, no chest-beating, no self-praise*

3. Send the newsletter out *irregularly*, about three to six times a year.
- *If you announce you'll put it out every two months, you'll have no flexibility to miss your publishing "deadline" even though it's self-imposed*
- *More than once every two months is more work than necessary, but fewer than three times a year is too little to keep your prospects warm*

4. Be sure to send copies of the newsletter to current clients first.
- *If it's not good enough for your current customers, it's not good enough for your prospects*
- *Give it to current clients a good week in advance of mailing it to prospects*

5. Every newsletter should be mailed *from* the executive at your firm who knows the prospect by first name. He or she is the prospect's "sponsor."

■ *The first time, include a cover letter, signed by the sponsor, with a handwritten P.S. of some sort*

■ *Subsequent newsletters should have the sponsor's business card or note clipped to it, with a handwritten notation about the contents ("Thought you'd be particularly interested in the article on widgets, p. 3. . . ." etc.)*

6. Whenever appropriate, include an offer in the newsletter for a more in-depth study, survey summary, or research report, just completed by your firm.

■ *Give prospects an opportunity to respond to the newsletter occasionally*

■ *Suggest a phone call to the sponsoring executive rather than a formal reply card or other "junk mail" device*

7. If more than one contact at a single company is to receive a mailing, in addition to personalizing the cover note, try to include different versions for each executive.

■ *Generate four or five versions of a cover letter, and use Version A as the primary vehicle*

- *If two executives at one company are to get the mailing, give one Version A and the other Version B, and so forth*
- *If twenty executives at a single company are receiving a mailing, it's not critical to have twenty versions, but be sure the four or five versions you have available are randomly used with all twenty contacts*

Making Friends of Noncustomers

There are lots of examples of this kind of marketing at work on the consumer side. Companies in all types of business are rediscovering the immense benefits of serving the interests of people who aren't even their customers yet, although frequently in consumer-oriented businesses a company doesn't really do any individualized "tracking" of prospect relationships.

My wife and I recently owned a Chevrolet Caprice station wagon. We liked the car but it was prone to flat tires. In the three years we owned it we had four flats. The last time our Chevy had a flat, we put the spare on and Pamela took it to a tire store, Townfair Tires in Fairfield, Connecticut.

Now, the truth is, she and I know nothing at all about cars or tires. She had driven on the tire for a few feet when it was totally flat and she was worried she might have ruined it. So she took it in to Townfair, asked them to tell her if they could fix it, and then went across the street to have a salad while they lined the car up for service.

She went back to Townfair forty minutes later, expecting to have to buy a new steel-belted tire at a hundred dollars or more. They said, "No, we fixed the tire. Everything's fine. The tire's great. It had a small nail hole, but repaired it. Now it's good as new, so we put it back on the car, and we put your spare back where it belongs."

Pamela said, "Great. How much do I owe you?"

"Nothing."

"Nothing?"

"Right, nothing."

"Not anything? Don't you charge . . ."

"We don't charge for fixing flat tires."

"Why?"

"Because we want your tire business, and we want you to remember us when you or your husband next shop for tires."

Townfair could easily have charged us for a totally new tire. We would have been happy to get off with having to pay only for fixing the flat. So why didn't they charge us?

Obviously, the people at Townfair know that while it doesn't cost much to repair a flat tire, it costs a lot to get a new customer. They are *giving away* a very simple form of service to gain what is potentially an immense amount of future business.

In our case, they were definitely successful. We'll be going back there anytime we need tires. We won't mind paying full price either, because we're quite confident we can trust these guys.

Here's another example. There's a clothing store in Westport called Mitchell's. Mitchell's also believes in high quality service. Their salespeople are not on commission, they're on salary. They develop their own clientele and are encouraged to send out personal notes, thank-yous, and so forth. These efforts are backed up by the store's management, which maintains a detailed customer database for the use of the sales staff. Altogether, a class act in retailing.

One recent Saturday I went to Mitchell's and saw a barbecue grill set up in front of the store, with a young man turning hot dogs over the fire.

Apparently they were selling hot dogs. What a great idea, I thought!

But they weren't selling hot dogs. They were giving them away. And not just to people who bought things or went into their store either. Anyone could drive into the parking lot, ask for a hot dog, and get one.

They must have had dozens of hot dogs on the grill, plus a full-time person out there serving them. It was simply a means of getting the attention of current and prospective customers for the time it took to let them know what kind of a store Mitchell's was. That's really all we're talking about here. It's a very, very common-sense technique.

Both these cases—and they're both consumer-oriented cases—illustrate the importance of giving small tokens of service away if you want to cultivate your crop of prospective customers or clients. You'll probably end up going to quite a bit of effort to maximize the number of prospects you make voice contact with. So now it's time to tend this crop carefully, so as not to lose any of the contacts you've worked so hard to make.

Step-by-Step Guide to Prospect Cultivation

1. Prospect cultivation can't be rushed. The people you make contact with will have to make their own decision, in their own time. You just want to be there, in their line of sight, when decision time comes. Hitting someone with a sales pitch every time you talk to them will actually be counterproductive, at least in most cases.

Also, no matter how much effort you put against a particular prospect, in most businesses you will have little impact on his timing. It really is like growing a crop, or having a baby. It takes nine months for a woman to have a baby. You can put nine women on it, but it will still take nine months.

2. Provide a service to your prospects as if they were your clients. The service you provide, in fact, whether it's a newsletter, an occasional research report, or some other vehicle, has to be good enough for your current clients! Be sure your current clients get their own versions of whatever service you're providing for your prospects.

3. Never miss an opportunity to make an additional personal contact with someone you already know. You don't have to shower people with attention, just let them know once in a while you haven't forgotten about them, you're still interested. If you're traveling anyway, make a few calls before a trip and see if you can take one of your contacts to lunch, or buy him a drink, while you're in town.

4. Look for and use news about your contacts. Scan the business pages for any mention of the names of any of your prospects. If you have a lot of contacts, arm an assistant with their names, and do a regular, weekly key-word search of all the obvious news and trade-news sources. When a contact of yours gets into the press, if it's appropriate you might want to call just to say you caught the reference, and congratulations. At a minimum, you can send out a note. A press mention is a wonderful excuse for a personal note.

If the press mention occurs because your contact is changing jobs, don't be disappointed. A contact who changes jobs creates a whole chain of opportunities. So call him at his new position and congratulate him. And, by the way, does he know who replaced him at the other firm? Can you or should you use his name when you call that person? Who had the position at this new firm before he got it? What happened to that person, where is she now? And so on, and so on . . .

5. Never denigrate your opponents. If the conversation swings around to your industry, the highest possible form of selling is to *compliment* your rivals. You don't need to carry it to an extreme, but if the subject comes up, don't succumb to the temptation to run down an opponent. That's what everyone would expect of you, it's completely predictable, it will therefore always lack credibility, and by succumbing you will miss an absolutely marvelous opportunity. By complimenting a competitor (sincerely, not with false praise), you automatically set your own firm at a higher, more objective level than the competitor.

6. Don't solve the prospect's problems. If your prospect brings a conversation around to a discussion of his own firm, and his own issues, your role is to offer a sounding board and to be sympathetic. If you leap in too soon to try to suggest helpful solutions, even though they may seem obvious to you, then you risk your credibility—particularly if a solution you suggest would involve doing business with your firm, or benefiting your company in any way. (Think about how you discuss your current spouse's ex with him. Or her.)

Your goal, in all contacts with a prospect, is to build the trust of that prospect. You want him to see you as totally objective, sympathetic, and sincerely concerned with the success of his business, whether or not you ever have a relationship with him.

Keep Your Perspective

While tending your crop of prospects, your goal should be to give every one of them a little taste of what it could mean to do business with you. Any kind of selling during the relationship management process is almost always going to be counter-productive. Instead, just by serving your prospects' interests you are also "selling" your firm to them, and you're selling it in the most persuasive, credible fashion possible.

The most effective kind of pitch is fashioned not just to get what you want, but to deliver what your prospect needs. The more you pay attention during the prospect cultivation process, the better you'll be able to determine and meet your prospect's needs when the time comes.

So don't try to do everything at once. Instead, concentrate on learning about your prospects, individually. Study each of them. Understand them.

If you want to persuade someone, first visualize what it would be like if you were where he is, doing what he does, thinking what he thinks.

It's a lot like life.

Solutions to Ethics Questionnaire

Sorry. There are no right answers. Surely you're not surprised?

▼▼▼▼▼▼▼

Acknowledgments

Success in any field is rarely a function of a single individual's capabilities, and my own career as a rainmaker has benefited immensely from the active help of a large number of friends and colleagues too numerous to name. There have been a few, however, from whom I've learned an extraordinary amount.

My boss for four years, Bob Schmidt, tops the list. CEO of Levine, Huntley, Schmidt and Beaver, Bob was one of the best "closers" in a pitch meeting that I've ever witnessed in action. You have to have a certain killer instinct to close a persuasive meeting with an irresistible appeal. He went right for the soft spot every time. And he did it very instinctively.

I found Bob to be a great guy to work for, because I never thought I was really working for him. You might say he was a noninterventionist. If I had a problem, I could go to him for help. If he had one, he'd find me. In between, both of us enjoyed a great deal of latitude.

Because of the freedom he gave me in my first advertising "new-business" position, I had a license to develop my own style of working, and that's what I did. Over time I developed my own set of guidelines—a checklist of things to do and not to do—which seemed to work. In subsequent jobs at other agencies and in my own business as a consultant, I've continued to practice—and to teach —these principles.

Special thanks, also, to Leslie Whitaker. Leslie helped organize the book and spun a lot of ramblings into gold. Without Leslie's immense contribution I probably would never have finished the project. But she helped me get it done the right way, on time, and in my own words. Thanks!

I owe a particularly large debt of gratitude to Patti Goldrick (now married, she goes by the name Patti Gormley). Although during most of our time together Patti worked for me, I'm not too sure even now if I wasn't really working for her. I often got the feeling that my own new-business triumphs were really her triumphs that I got to take credit for.

In any good salesperson you can usually spot a certain degree of optimistic self-deception. A good salesperson really believes he can win, even when he's almost certain to lose. He can keep going in the face of an onslaught of setbacks and negative news. The more optimistic and indefatigable a salesperson is, the more successful he is likely to be. But self-deception, when practiced on such a continuous basis, can easily become self-delusion.

Patti Goldrick was the one who would bring me back to the real world when my salesperson's optimism got out of hand. Patti was my lifeline to reality.

Life's a Pitch is largely based on my life as an advertising pitchman. I've punctuated it with anecdotes from my own experience, pitching large and small companies, household names and unknown entrepreneurs. I did my best to recall each of these situations accurately, but occasionally my salesperson's optimism—my success-oriented self-deception—may have played tricks on my memory. My apologies in advance for any inaccuracies.

Finally, I'd like to thank Laurie Coots at Chiat/Day in Los Angeles. Laurie is a terrific new-business executive in her own right, but also a great team player. I enjoyed working with her the few times I had the opportunity, but I want to thank her particularly for the title of this book. In the dull after-ache of one particularly grueling and unsuccessful pitch, Laurie distributed consolation T-shirts to all of us, on which were printed the words:

LIFE'S A PITCH. THEN YOU DIE.

▼▼▼▼▼▼▼

Index

▼▼▼▼▼▼▼

About the Author

Don Peppers has spent the last fifteen years in a variety of business-development positions in and around the world of marketing and advertising.

According to *The New York Times,* his track record of successful pitches has made him "one of the advertising industry's best-known scouts for new business." And *The Wall Street Journal* commented that "Mr. Peppers . . . helped make new-business hunting one of the most glamorous fields in the ad business."

Don is also the coauthor, with Dr. Martha Rogers, of *The One to One Future: Building Relationships One Customer at a Time,* (New York: Currency/Doubleday, 1993).

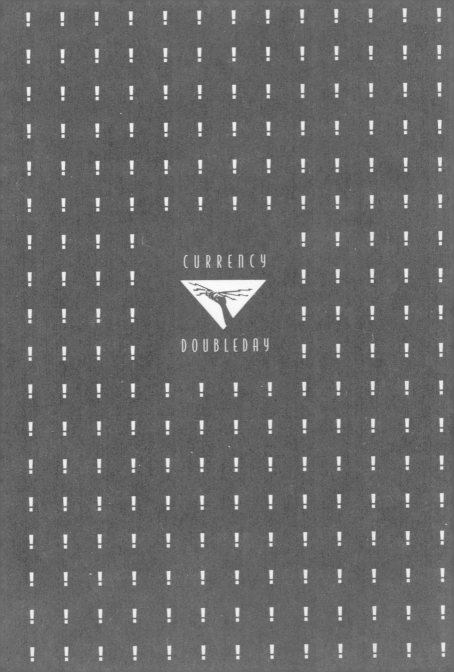

CURRENCY

DOUBLEDAY